TRAVELS

OF

ROBERT AND SARAH LINDSEY.

ILLUSTRATED BY

ROBERT LINDSEY CLARK,

AFTER ORIGINAL SKETCHES

BY

FREDERIC MACKIE.

EDITED BY

ONE OF THEIR DAUGHTERS.

LONDON:

SAMUEL HARRIS AND CO., 5, BISHOPSGATE WITHOUT.

—

1886.

PREFACE.

In selecting the following extracts from my parents' journals, and preparing a short sketch of their early and latter days, I have been induced to do so from a belief that their grandchildren especially, and some relatives and friends who hold their memory in loving regard, would be pleased to have some record of their long and distant travels.

It may be thought that such a book should have been printed long ago ; but circumstances seem to have forbidden its execution until now ; and notwithstanding the years that have elapsed since the events related took place, it is hoped that the interest of the following pages may not be thereby greatly diminished.

E. L. G.

6th of 3rd month, 1886.

CONTENTS.

—

ILLUSTRATIONS.

EARLY LIFE.

ROBERT LINDSEY was born at Gildersome, in Yorkshire, in 1801. His father, Richard Lindsey, had married Mary Cooper, of Brighouse, and his paternal ancestors for two generations further back also bore the name of Richard Lindsey, and lived at Gildersome. My grandfather was a woollen cloth manufacturer in partnership with his brother, and traded a good deal with America. He went over to that country on business in 1811, in order to recover debts which were owing to him, and spent three years there, during which time the United States declared war against Great Britain, and he was taken prisoner, suspected of being a British spy, and conducted by armed soldiers for trial before two of their officers. After having satisfied themselves of his innocence, he was detained for some days a prisoner on parole; the reason given by the colonel and major being, that the British had detained several American subjects, and they believed they had a right to act in retaliation. They treated him however with kindness and consideration, and after the repeated intercessions of some of his friends, he was told that the British having released a captain of an American vessel would operate in his favour; and after consultation with a superior officer, he was set at liberty on condition he would swear or affirm that he would not take up arms against the United

States, or otherwise interfere in warlike measures, that being the ground on which the before-mentioned person had been liberated by the British.

My father spent about three years at Ackworth school, and afterwards went to a school at Darlington, kept by Joseph Samms. A few letters written by him at this time may not be uninteresting.

Ackworth, 23rd 12th month, 1812.

DEAR FATHER,

* * * * I am at present learning compound proportion in vulgar fractions. There has lately been a great fall of snow, and now our chief play is sliding, which keeps us warm. I suppose there is plenty of snow and ice in North America, and I dare say it is as much too cold in winter as it is too hot in summer. I like my situation. I should be very glad to have another letter from thee, and let me know when thou intendest to come home. I have lately begun to learn geography, which I like pretty well. * * * In my last letter I forgot to tell thee that I was very much obliged to thee for the book thou sentest me, entitled Lady Guion's Poems, which is a very instructive book, and I like it very well. With dear love I conclude, and remain thy affectionate son,

ROBERT LINDSEY.

Ackworth, 25th 3rd month, 1814.

DEAR PARENTS,

I received father's acceptable letter. It gave me great pleasure to be informed of his safe return from America. It was also pleasant to learn that you, sisters, and other relations at Gildersome were pretty well. I was much obliged to you for the parcel which you sent me along with the letter, and should be glad to have another letter from you; but I should be still more so to see my father again after a long absence of upwards of three years, * * * I am learning simple equations in algebra. Two of our masters, viz., John Donbavand and Samuel Evens, together with William Adamson, the houseman, went to the house of correction at Wakefield, on the 18th day of this month, to undergo a month's confinement for refusing to serve in the militia. We have had a very severe winter; but the weather is growing milder, so that the boys are pretty busy in their gardens sowing seeds, &c. * * * With dear love to you, sisters, grandmother, and other relations, I still remain to be affectionately your son,

ROBERT LINDSEY.

Darlington, 11th mo. 23rd, 1815.

DEAR PARENTS,

I have to acknowledge father's letter of last month. * * * I have lately been mostly employed in learning the languages, but master thought to employ a little of my time in some parts of the day in studying Euclid's Elements would be of considerable advantage to me, as tending to expand my mind, and being a little relief from too close attention to the other studies. I have some time ago finished navigation. Master thinks that the reading of the book you sent me would not be of much use at present, unless it were a selection of what there is in it, as he fears there are several things in it rather improper for boys at school to read. * * * Please to be so kind as to tell cousin Hannah Lindsey that master does not inspect the letters that are sent us as at Ackworth, so that I think she might write a few lines as soon as convenient, as I should much like to hear from her. Master desires me to give his and mistress's kind love to you. I don't know anything more to write, so shall conclude with love to you, sisters, and grandmother, and remain,

Your affectionate son,

ROBERT LINDSEY.

A letter from his father in America shows how carefully he was watched over in his youthful days :—

Quebec, 28th 10th mo., 1811.

MY DEAR ROBERT,

Thy letter to me dated 8th of 8th month is received, brought by the vessel called the "Britannia," which arrived safely at this port after a passage of nearly ten weeks from Liverpool. On reading thy letter I am pleased to observe thy improvement in writing since I left home, by which I am also inclined to hope thou hast also improved in reading, to which branch of learning I wish particularly to turn thy attention at present, and have no doubt that if thou sufficiently attends to thy master's instructions in this respect (and hope thou wilt be very careful to do so), thou wilt soon learn to read as well as to speak with propriety. I desire thee to make a practice of reading to thy mother at any time when thou hast an opportunity of being in her company. If thou art still at John Ellis's school on the receipt of this letter, I have particularly to desire thee to be very careful and mindful in strictly following and attending to the directions and instructions which may from time to time be given thee by John and Mary Ellis, as well as by their daughters Sarah and Eliza, and it will be a satisfaction and pleasure to me when I hear of that being the case; at the same time I shall be much grieved to hear anything to the contrary on thy account, but which I do hope will not be. Now with regard to thy conduct towards the other boys, I must desire thee to be very much on thy guard, and exceedingly careful not to offend any of them in word or deed; and even should it happen that any of them should offend thee by any means, or do anything to thee which thou may think wrong, do not be angry, but endeavour to bear it with patience, and rather show a kind disposition towards them than otherwise, or at least go out of their way, and be always ready to convince them that thou art willing to return good for evil. Before I close my letter, there is one thing I wish to impress on thy mind, and that is never to suffer a single word to come out of thy mouth which is not strictly true. When thou writes to me again take only half a sheet of thin paper, and rule thy lines very closely. Thou must consider that paper is expensive, but the postage is still more expensive for large letters.

RICHARD LINDSEY.

His father intended him for the medical profession, and it appears to have been a disappointment to him that his son could not fall in with his wishes in this respect, but my father believed he was not fitted for the life of a doctor; and he was finally apprenticed at Thirsk to learn the drapery business. He began business for himself in the manufacturing village of Brighouse, in Yorkshire, when about twenty-four years of age, and at twenty-seven he married Sarah Crosland, of Bolton, in Lancashire.

A few extracts from my mother's private memoranda respecting her early life, throw some light on her character and religious experience.

"Having at various seasons written a few memoranda in commemoration of the Lord's dealings with me from my youth, I feel disposed at this time to revise them and make some further additions thereto.

"I was born on the 1st of 4th month, 1804, and was the second daughter of Robert and Mary Crosland, of Bolton, in Lancashire. My mother's maiden name was Hall, and her birthplace Manchester. My father's parents were valued elders in the Society of Friends, and lived at Oldfieldnook, near Brighouse. In looking back at my youthful days, I am bound to confess that the fruits of our fallen nature were often predominant, and I was many times inclined to rebel against those restrictions which my dear mother found it needful to lay upon me. I had a high spirit, and often gave way to passion. I possessed great sensibility, and well remember a season when I was about nine years old, some of my brothers and myself were sitting round the fire with our dear mother, and one of the party reading an account of the dissolute life and unhappy death of an unfortunate youth, which had such an effect upon my mind that I could not forbear weeping, and exposing myself to those around me.

"In the winter of the year 1815 my dear mother died, leaving seven children, I being the second. On retiring to rest one night (I believe it was the last of my mother's life), I had a most delightful dream, which had such an effect upon my mind that I incline to record it. I thought I was in a room filled with angels, who were flying about in all directions, and making the most delightful music, far transcending anything I had ever heard on earth, and quite unintelligible to me; and on making enquiry as to the meaning of it, I was informed that these angelic creatures were come to conduct my dear mother to heaven.

"When I was thirteen years of age my dear father married a second time, and we met with a kind caretaker in the woman of his choice, Esther Wood, of Bolton, by whom he had six children. She died in the meridian of life.

"In the year 1827 I became acquainted with Robert Lindsey, of Brighouse, whose mother was my father's second cousin, and we were married in the ninth month of the following year. In my dear husband I found all that my heart could desire as regarded many things; yet I was often sad; and for some years after our marriage I feared we were not making much progress towards the kingdom of heaven, and as our family increased I thought my dearest earthly treasure was too much taken up with the lawful pleasures of this life, and the Holy Spirit seemed in danger of being buried in my own heart. It was often impressed upon my mind that I must not set my affections too much upon my dear husband, but consider him as a treasure lent, to be returned at the Lord's will. I sometimes found it to be my duty to express a few words to my dearest earthly treasure relative to my fears; but this was always greatly in the cross to my own will, and the enemy endeavoured to dissuade me from doing so, and insinuated that if I gave up to say all to him that might be required, he would not receive it in love, that I should live very uncomfortably with him * * * I now began to doubt whether I had done right in marrying, and I begged of my Heavenly Father that if I had missed my way in this respect, He would still condescend to be with me, and to make me a vessel for his own use in some shape or other. * * * After this I felt as if struggling with the powers of darkness for a few days, until at length light broke forth, and my darkness became as the noonday; and my Heavenly Father was mercifully pleased to show me with undoubted clearness that I was given as a help meet to my dear husband, and intended as an instrument to bring him nearer to the ever-blessed truth, and that he was a chosen vessel for the Lord's use, to be brought forth in due season, and my mental eye saw him standing in the preachers' gallery in a Friends' meeting; and, on looking towards myself, the prospect seemed so clear and cloudless that I was ready to conclude my work was finished, and that I had not much longer to remain in the body; and for some days the language of Holy Writ was much upon my mind, ' Arise, shine, for thy light is come, and the glory of the Lord is risen upon thee.' Then things appeared to wear a different aspect, and I seemed in some degree like one who had risen from the dead; old things appeared to have passed away, and all things to have become new. It was in the spring of the year 1833 that my heavenly Father thus condescended to bring me up out of the miry clay, to set my feet upon a rock, and put a new song into my mouth, even praises to His holy name. * * * The two or three years following were seasons of much anxiety, on account of an increasing family, and our business, which in former years had supported us,

beginning to decline; so that, on making up our yearly
accounts, our expenses more than once exceeded our
income, and, as no way opened for a change, our faith
was often deeply tried. We endeavoured to use strict
economy in all things until the close of the year 1843,
when my grandfather, James Hall, died, aged ninety-four
years. He commenced the world with slender means,
but by his own industry made a handsome fortune, and I,
along with my brothers and sisters, came in for a share
of it, which placed us in more easy circumstances; and,
having known the reverse, I trust our hearts overflowed
with gratitude to the Giver of everything which we enjoyed. * * * In the 12th month, 1844, my dear husband
having obtained a certificate from his Monthly Meeting,
left home to visit the families of Friends in the com-
pass of Manchester Meeting, which occupied him several
weeks. * * * In the third month of the following year
my R. L. left home again to pay a similar visit to the
families of Friends within Liverpool Meeting.

"In the 5th month of 1845 my dear father died from
an apoplectic seizure, under which he lingered for more
than a week, aged seventy-two years. This afflictive
event was the means of further increasing our income.
Soon afterwards, my dear husband, thinking he might
have to leave home again on religious service, and not
liking to leave me burdened with the business, proposed
our giving it up, and retiring to a private house, which
proposition I did not at first fall in with, as we had then
six children, and it appeared to me unlikely for a man
with a large family to give up his business in the meridian
of life with only slender means; and it was no small
trial of my faith; but, after considering the subject, I
felt most easy to yield to it. Accordingly, the drapery
business was resigned, and we removed to another house
in the village, much pains being taken to make our house
and garden pleasant. But this rest was of short dura-
tion, as in the second month of 1846, at our Monthly
Meeting at Brighouse, my R. L. informed his friends

that his mind had been drawn towards paying a visit to the Friends in Ireland, for which service, after due consideration, he was liberated, and was absent from home about three months, during which time he attended the Yearly Meeting in Dublin, and visited the families of Friends in many places in the eastern and southern provinces. In two months after, at our Monthly Meeting at Bradford, my dear husband opened a prospect to his friends which he said had been before him for seven years, which was that it would be required of him to offer himself as a companion to Benjamin Seebohm in a religious visit which he was going to pay to the Friends in North America. The subject was solemnly considered, and united with * * * The needful preparations were hastily made, and they embarked at Liverpool. My dear husband and self kept up a regular correspondence during his absence in America, and I was generally cheered with letters once a fortnight, which tended to brighten that chain of love and conjugal affection which bound us together in our youthful days.

"In the 4th month, 1849, I was made sensible that a renewed call was extended towards me, and the time seemed to be come for me to bind those sacrifices to the horns of the altar which I had had in prospect for about nine years, during which time some sacrifices, chiefly in meetings for discipline, had been called for. But now the time appeared to be come to put on strength in the name of the Lord. My communications were generally short, and sometimes very mortifying to flesh and blood; and, if the Lord's hand had not been underneath, surely I should have fallen under discouragement. In this year our income, which with care and frugality had supplied our needful wants, was more than doubled in consequence of the death of a relative, which laid us under renewed obligations to devote ourselves and our all to the disposal of Him who had given us all things richly to enjoy.

"My dear husband returned home in 1851, after an

absence of four and three-quarter years. * * * But our blissful union was of short continuance, and we were soon to part again, our cup too. full. We were busily engaged with workmen for several months making alterations in. our dwelling house and premises ; and in the 2nd month of 1852, at our Monthly Meeting at Brighouse, my dear husband opened a concern which had come before him whilst in America, to pay a visit in Gospel love to Friends and those in connection with them in Van Dieman's Land, Australia, New Zealand, &c."

We now go back to my father's setting out on his first journey to America, and extracts from the journal he kept during his absence will describe his life whilst there.

AMERICAN JOURNEY.

In the 10th month of 1846 my father set sail from Liverpool with Benjamin Seebohm, whose companion he was going to be, on a religious visit to North America. They landed at Boston, and soon proceeded to New York, and from thence to Philadelphia, where they made their home at Marmaduke C. Cope's, in Filbert Street. My father was much pleased to renew the acquaintance of his cousins, Joseph Sharp and wife, whom he had not seen for twenty years. They were mutually glad to see each other. Several Friends called to see B. S. and R. L., and they paid several visits to Friends in the city. My father in his journal speaks of attending Haddonfield Quarterly Meeting:—

"17th 12 mo.—The weather this day was very winterly, the snow falling nearly the whole of it, which no doubt prevented some Friends getting out to the Quarterly Meeting; but it was pleasant to see it so well attended, notwithstanding the roughness of the morning. There were upwards of a hundred carriages standing in the yard, and we were told there were a considerable number at the inn in the village, so that I suppose there might be at least a hundred and fifty altogether. There is a very busy scene witnessed at the close of the meeting, carriages starting off in various directions over the country. It is also pleasant to see what good accommodation is provided adjoining their meeting houses for the horses and carriages. They all seem to drive, even if it is for a short distance. Walking seems to be out of the question with them."

The Friends in Philadelphia were at this time in a very divided and inharmonious state, and it was very trying for B. S. and my father to attend their meetings, and come into social contact with many of them. B. S. proposed to two of the Monthly Meetings in Philadelphia to visit their families, but his offer was rejected twice. They now visited many of the smaller meetings in Pennsylvania, and others at no great distance:—

"On 7th day morning, accompanied by our kind landlord, M. C. Cope, we went to Westown, where Friends of this Yearly Meeting have established a boarding school for both sexes. It has been in operation since the beginning of the present century, and seems to be well conducted. The children receive a good education, and are well cared for in every respect. The charge is eighty dollars a year, and the premises are calculated to contain about two hundred and fifty boys and girls; although it scarcely seems correct to call them so, as they have no restriction in respect to age, and there are a large proportion of both sexes more advanced to man and womanhood than it is usual to see in any school in England. We understood that many of them were from eighteen to twenty years of age. It is the practice for some of them to be at school in the winter, and at home with their parents in the summer months, to assist in the business of the farm, which seems to be the reason of their being so much further advanced in years before leaving school than is the case with us."

27th of 3rd mo., 1847.—Set out for Stroudsburgh. My father's journal says:—

"Our road for the first few miles lay on the banks of the Delaware, the hill along the edge of the river rising to a considerable height, being cut away sufficiently to afford two carriages to pass, and in some places barely so. The scenery was very bold; but the wind being pretty high, suggested something of fear to my mind, lest our carriage should be blown over. But we were favoured to reach a tavern in safety, fourteen miles on our way, where we dined, and about two o'clock set off again. Considerable snow had fallen, and in many places it was drifted, so as to render it difficult for our horses to get along, and the more so as the wind was very high, and blew the snow in clouds, so as many times to hinder our seeing far before us. In some places large trees were blown down, and lay across the road, so as to render it needful for us to go through the woods in order to pass them, so that our getting on was attended with considerable difficulty. About four o'clock we came up to the pass through the Blue Mountains called the ' Delaware Water Gap,' a very remarkable chasm or opening through which the river passes, the mountains on each side being not less than ten or twelve hundred feet in height. The road is cut along the edge of the river through the fissure for the distance of about three miles, and the mountains on each side, although very steep, are in many places clothed with low pines and mountain laurels, which, with the huge masses of rock jutting out here and there, give it a very striking appearance, if we add to this the rapid waters of the river, agitated by the wintry winds which were blowing wildly round us. I believe there are many like myself, unaccustomed to such dangers, who would feel it a relief when they were safely passed, which we were favoured to see through the protecting care of Him who formed these stupendous mountains, and to reach the Friend's house where we were expected to lodge. * * *

"3rd mo. 29th.—The last two or three days' journeys we have passed many saw mills, situated on the creeks and mountain streams, a considerable business being carried on in this part of the country in what is called 'lumbering,' that is, in cutting down the forest trees, sawing them into boards or planks, and rafting them in this state down the Lehigh, Susquehanna, and Delaware rivers, for sale and exportation from the seaports.

"3rd mo. 30th, 1847.—This morning left Stoddardsville, a small town situated on the Lehigh river, and rode over the Broad Mountains eighteen miles to Wilksbarre, the capital town of the county of Luzerne, on the east bank of the Susquehanna, which is here crossed by a long wooden bridge, over which we passed after dining at Wilksbarre, and had a romantic drive of twelve miles between a high range of hills along the Susquehanna, which is here a noble stream, in many parts not less than three hundred or four hundred yards wide. About dusk we reached Wolf's Tavern, situated on the edge of the river, and stopped for the night. Though this was only a small house compared with many, I was struck in seeing the variety of dishes they placed on the table for supper and breakfast, including, amongst other things, wild pigeons, of which within a few days we have seen very large flocks passing over our heads. We understand they are taken in large numbers by nets, as well as shot with the rifle.

"Muncy, 4th mo. 2nd.—The afternoon was fine. Our friend Jacob Haines went with us as guide, and we got on very pleasantly for about ten miles, until we reached the summit of the Alleghany Range, when we had a very beautiful sight of the setting sun, after which we descended the north side of the mountain, where the snow lay a considerable thickness in many places, and the road being very narrow, cut out of the mountain side, only just of sufficient width for a carriage to pass along, it required the utmost skill of our driver to keep in the path, as well as the assistance of our guide to keep the carriage up behind, to prevent its being overturned and thrown down the precipice below, which in many parts was of great depth beneath us. Notwithstanding all our care, the wheels slid off the path at one point, and it was with the exertion of all parties that we were able to get it up again, but this was accomplished; and at another place, in passing over a very narrow bridge, one of the wheels got off the side, and from the bad foothold which our horses had in the snow, one of them lost his feet in coming down a declivity, but was enabled to recover himself pretty speedily, so that it was felt to be renewed cause of thankfulness to our great Caretaker, when we were favoured to reach our place of rest for the night.

" 4th mo. 3rd.— * * * About eleven o'clock we left Hillsgrove for Elklands. Our road lay through the woods, and on our way we passed a family who were engaged in making sugar from the juice of the maple tree, which is abundant in this part of the country and grows to a large size. They tap the tree, and sap exudes out slowly, and is caught in small wooden troughs placed there for the purpose. It has very much the appearance of clear water, and has not much taste. It is boiled down to a consistency either for molasses or sugar in large iron kettles hung on a pole over a fire of wood. The party whom we passed readily offered us some of the syrup, which we found to be very delicious. We reached a Friend's house at Elklands about three o'clock with considerable difficulty over the worst road I ever passed, after breaking one of the swingle trees of our carriage, which was quickly repaired by cutting down a sapling in the wood, and making one which answered our present need very well. We had taken an axe with us, which we found to be a common practice in this part of the country; trees not unfrequently falling across the road, which have to be cut away before a carriage can pass. Our road this day was strewed all around with large tim- ber trees, blown or cut down, and going to decay; and what added very much to the desolation of the scene,

were numerous large dead trunks of trees standing, which
had been girdled, that is, the bark cut round about two
feet from the ground, and left in that state to wither
away, merely to save the trouble and expense of cutting
them down. * * * Uncleared land, that is land covered
with timber the growth of ages, may be purchased in the
neighbourhood of Elklands at one dollar per acre. The
usual plan in clearing is to cut the trees down about two
feet above the ground, and leave the stumps to decay,
which takes many years to do, particularly with some
sorts of timber. They plough between the stumps, which,
although troublesome to a stranger, we understand those
who are accustomed to it do without much inconvenience.
It has a singular appearance to see a field dotted over
pretty thickly with old stumps, which with us would be
thought very much in the way, but here it would not pay
to be at the expense of removing them.

" 5th mo. 5th.—As we passed through the woods this
morning we observed the ravages of a fire which had
prevailed for many miles a few days before, and had very
much destroyed the appearance of vegetation where it
had passed, leaving little but the blackened and charred
trunks of the pine standing. The keeper of a tavern
where we called, said they could hear the roar of the fire
at the distance of three miles. A fall of rain seemed to
have checked its progress after it had raged for two or
three days. * * * On our way this afternoon my mind
was introduced into very close conflict from the fresh
opening of a field of service, which I had seen in the
vision of that light which maketh manifest all things,
even things to come, since setting my feet on these
shores, and at the sight of which my very heart has been
ready to sink within me. It was this day more indelibly
impressed upon my mind as the path of peace for me;
and it was also shown me that if I am favoured faithfully to follow the Lord in the way of his requirings, my
time for the next few years must be very much, if not

altogether, devoted to the service of Truth; after which, if the Lord should see meet to lengthen my days, it was given me to believe I should be permitted to pass the evening of my life as in the bosom of my family, patiently waiting and quietly hoping for the salvation of my God, who hath been with me and followed me with the reproofs and instructions of his Good Spirit to this day. * * *

"6th mo. 24th, 1847, Philadelphia.—This afternoon took a drive out of the city about six miles to Laurel Hill Cemetery, a beautiful place on the banks of the Schuylkill, to see the last resting place of the remains of Uncle William Lindsey, my father's only brother, who died about eight years ago, and lies interred there. I went in company with cousins Hannah Sharp and Joseph Lindsey, and several others of the family, and was much pleased with the place and the scenery about it. The grounds are laid out with great taste, and are kept in very nice order.

"6th mo. 30th.—This morning, after taking an affectionate leave of several of our dear Friends in Philadelphia, unto whom we had become closely united, we left the city in company with our kind friend William Tatum, who was very agreeably our companion and caretaker through Jersey, and again freely tendered his services in our journey out to Ohio, which was very acceptable to us, and it has felt to me to be cause of thankfulness that we are so suitably provided in this respect. Indeed it is more than could be looked for by us, to observe the willingness and readiness of Friends wherever our lot has been cast to serve us, poor and unworthy as we feel ourselves to be.

"First day, 7th mo. 4th.—This afternoon I spent very much in my own chamber, as did also my companions, esteeming it no small privilege to have the opportunity to retire a few hours to commune in secret with my past

c

hours, although in so doing my heart is often sad under the conviction of the very little progress I have made in the great and important work of the day, in preparation for heaven; for I am abundantly convinced that my heart is not so set on things above as becomes the disciple of the lowly Jesus, who had not, when on earth, whereon to lay His head. I feel my want of love to Him as the altogether lovely of the redeemed soul, as the chief of ten thousand. I feel the need of His reigning without a rival in my heart, so that for His sake I should not only willingly, but joyfully suffer. I am jealous lest I should be deceiving myself; for if I had indeed put on Christ, it would be my meat and drink to do and to suffer the will of my Father who is in heaven. But instead of this, how doth my weak heart tremble and faint at the prospect of the path which the Lord hath increasingly opened to my view, in the fulfilment of which it will be required of me to forsake all, and to follow Him as unto the uttermost parts of the earth. So close does this feel to my nature, that it is truly like dividing as between the joints and marrow." * * *

My father felt the continued separation from his beloved wife very keenly, and often were his prayers put up to his Heavenly Father on her behalf, and on that of his dear children, that the Lord would keep and preserve them on every hand, and be a father to the fatherless and a husband to the widow. He often underwent deep conflicts of spirit, when Satan presented temptations and suggested doubts and difficulties, almost leading at times to despair. But on turning his mind to God for help in his distress, he never failed to know the tempter silenced and the tempest stilled by the power of Him who said to the troubled waters, " Peace, be still."

"10th mo. 4th.—* * * We crossed the Ohio river in both its branches at Pittsburgh, and six miles beyond stopped for the night at a very comfortable tavern, having travelled thirty-six miles in the course of the day. We took supper soon after we got to our quarters, which the landlady spread out for us very liberally, although it was only a small house, and she had very little assistance, waiting upon us herself with peculiar cheerfulness. The table was literally covered with good things, there being no less than ten different sorts of sweetmeats, four kinds of bread, and three sorts of animal food, besides tea and milk and et ceteras. This was more than we often meet with, yet everywhere this is a plentiful country.

"10th mo. 12th.—This morning the weather was cold and frosty. We got off in pretty good time, and had a tedious mountain ride over two or three ridges of the Alleghany range, only making sixteen miles before noon, though we were on the national road. About three miles after we started we entered Maryland, one of the slave-holding states, and at the tavern where we stopped to dine, I saw the first slave that I ever beheld, as far as I know. He was a youth of about sixteen, employed as a household servant. He seemed pretty comfortable, said he got plenty to eat and drink, but should prefer being free. * * * The forests at this season have a beautifully variegated appearance, the foliage displaying almost every shade, from the faded brown leaf which we see in England to the bright orange and the deep scarlet and crimson. * * * We stopped for the night at an inn where we seemed to get into the very atmosphere of slavery, the servants being all of that class, and all things about the house in keeping with what we may suppose would be the result of a system so fraught with evil as is this scourge of the human race. I think I pity the slave-holder as much as the slave, and consider them both as claiming the sympathy and feeling of their fellow-townsmen in no small degree.

"10th mo. 14th.—Last night we were comfortably accommodated at Vanhorn's Tavern, where no slaves were kept. The difference was very striking between this and the one where we stopped the previous night, the balance being very much in favour of free labour.

"Baltimore, 10th mo. 22nd.—This afternoon we went to look through the establishment of Hope Slatter, a noted slave merchant of this city. He showed us through the jail where he keeps them until he gets a sufficient number for a cargo, when he ships them to the south. He told us he had recently sent off a hundred and twenty. Their place of confinement was clean, and they seemed well fed and well clothed. Still they were slaves, liable to be bought and sold like cattle; and it was sickening to look upon them, our fellow-creatures, and to think that they were the property of their fellow-man, and that their destiny was the cotton plantation of the south, there to toil out their days under a burning sun, beneath the lash of the driver.

"11th mo. 3rd.—The man at whose house we were entertained last night owns a considerable number of slaves, and the effects of the system were, I thought, the most visible here of any place where we had been. He had a large tract of land, some of it of good quality, and a fine establishment; but things were much out of order, and showed the want of the master's personal attention. All seemed to be done by slave labour, neither the master nor mistress lifting a hand to do anything that could be done for them. They seemed to be the most really in bondage, for want of their energies of body and mind being called into healthy action. I think of the two, the evil is greater to the master than to the slave."

At the close of the Yearly Meeting at New Garden, North Carolina:—

"It has been an interesting sight to watch Friends setting out to their respective homes this morning, some in large covered waggons with four horses, and various kinds of carriages. Many of these have to go as much as from one to two hundred miles, and some three hundred, and expect to be from three and four days to a week on the road. They mostly bring their own provisions with them, and get lodging on the way at private houses as they can, and as they have no turnpikes to pay, they can travel at little expense.

"1st mo. 28th.—Left Proctor's Tavern about half-past seven, and reached the meeting house at Gravelly Run about eleven, having had bad roads, and myself a providential escape from a serious accident. I had ex-changed seats with our guide, Robert Binford, he having taken my place in the carriage which Benjamin was driving, and I was driving in his ' sulky,' which was drawn by a spirited horse, when the traces by some means got loose. The horse went on, the shafts of the vehicle fell to the ground, and I was thrown out; but the road being sandy, I received no injury. The horse, having got clear of the ' sulky,' instead of dashing on as I expected to see him at full speed, when he got up to the other carriage stopped very quietly, and allowed me to lay hold of him. On examining the ' sulky,' we found that the shafts were splintered, but not so as to render us unable to go forward; and this appeared to be nearly all the damage that was sustained by what might have been a fearful accident.

"29th.—Set out from Gravelly Run early this morn-ing, and came on to Richmond, thirty-three miles, where we arrived about four o'clock, and took up our quarters at Micajah Bates'. The bridge across James' River, upon which the town is situated, having been swept away by a flood about two months ago, we had to cross at a ferry close to the town, where we were in great danger of

another more fearful accident than the one which befell
me yesterday. Benjamin had driven on to the flat, when
by some means the horses, in being placed as the boatmen wished them to be, more in the middle of the boat,
got into the river, whither they would undoubtedly have
dragged the carriage also, had it not been that the side
of the flat, being somewhat higher than usual, prevented
its going over. The horses, after struggling awhile, broke
the pole asunder from the carriage, and being thus providentially set free, they made to the shore, and were
saved. One of the axletrees was also broken, and this,
in addition to the breakage of the pole, seemed to be all
the damage that was sustained. We had great reason
to mark the preserving Hand of our Heavenly Father in
this event, and to ascribe unto Him the tribute of thanksgiving for it.

" 2nd mo. 9th, 1848.—Set out pretty early this morning, intending to take the steamboat at Aquia Creek for
Washington, as it seemed likely to save us about seventy
miles of land travelling, but on reaching Fredericsburgh
about ten o'clock we were informed that the boat started
between twelve and one, and we were then twelve or
fourteen miles distant, and the road very indifferent and
not easy to find. We were without guide, as we had been
since leaving Cedar Creek, but we got directions as well
as we could, and set out, hoping with diligence to get
there in time; but we found the road more intricate and
worse than anything we had ever witnessed, so that it
was marvellous we got along without upsetting. We had
nevertheless the misfortune to catch the top of our carriage against the branch of a tree that had partly fallen
across the road, which not only damaged it considerably
but hindered us. This, together with losing our way two
or three times, put it out of our power to get in time for
the sailing of the boat, and when we got within sight
of the river and hoped to reach a place of rest for our
wearied horses, we seemed to come to the end of our

road, and found that there was a salt marsh between us
and our place of destination, through which it was impossible for us to pass. We were utterly at a loss which
way to turn, when at a distance we saw two or three
men to whom we called, and on one of them coming up
he told us we were on the right road to Aquia Creek, but
there was no way to it for our carriage ; but that we
must go back a little way to get on to the line of railroad
which we had followed for several miles from Fredericsburgh, and which we had seen the cars passing along on
their way to the same steamboat which we were aiming
to catch ; and he then instructed us to loose our horses
from the carriage, lead them up on the railroad to the
depôt, and get a truck from thence to fetch our carriage.
All which we did according to his directions, and were at
last favoured to reach the end of an eventful and dangerous day's journey, with no other damage than what our
carriage top had sustained, which we were able to repair
so as not to be much disadvantage. We found that we
should have to wait till to-morrow noon, and were glad
to find a good inn at the Railway Depôt, where both
ourselves and our poor horses could be comfortably accommodated. * * * The railroad and steamboat establishment is most beautifully situated at the junction of
Aquia Creek with the Potomac River, which is here a
noble stream of a mile or two in width, affording fine
navigation up to the metropolis of the United States. * *

" 2nd mo. 10th.—A beautifully fine morning. The
sun rising like a globe of fire on the waters of the noble
Potomac, which stretches out as far as the eye can reach
from the windows of our lodging-room towards the south-
east. * * * About noon left Aquia Creek in the ' Mount
Vernon' steamboat for the city of Washington, and had
a delightful sail up the Potomac, passing on our way
the residence and burial-place of the far-famed George
Washington, which seemed to be an object of interest to
all on board, not only to us who were strangers. We

likewise passed the town of Alexandria, about ten miles below Washington, and reached the city about four o'clock, having a fine view of it from the river for several miles. It is beautifully situated, and commands apparently all the advantages requisite for the metropolis of a great nation, but still it does not seem to have made the progress which no doubt its founder supposed it would have done before this time. * * * We took a walk to the Capitol, a noble building, worthy of its object, as the place of deliberation of the representatives of a powerful and growing Republic.

" Sixth day 11th.—This morning before breakfast took a walk down the Pennsylvania Avenue as far as the President's house, and walked through the grounds at the front of the house, from which there is an extensive prospect. * * *

" Philadelphia, 25th 3rd mo. 1848.—In the afternoon attended the funeral of cousin Joseph Sharp, aged fifty-four years. He was interred in the Western burying ground in this city, a numerous company of Friends being present on the occasion.

" 6th mo. 6th, 1848.—The birthday of my youngest child, who this day completes her fifth year. Oh! the many and varied scenes it hath been my lot to pass through since the day that this sweet pledge of our mutual love was given into the arms of its tender mother! and my heart glowed with delight as I gazed on the wife of my bosom at that most interesting moment, with feelings only understood by the loving and affectionate husband. Though the recollection of these moments is in some degree painful and most tenderly touching to my nature, in the sensible remembrance that I am now far removed from these dear objects of a husband's and a father's love, yet are they dear to memory. Still does my beating heart love to trace these scenes of days that

are passed, and to linger in spirit over the tender enjoy-
ments of conjugal and parental felicity which have been
granted me in my passage through time, and which have
again and again sweetened the bitter cup of life. And
oh! Thou bountiful Author of all our blessings, who,
unworthy as I am of the very least of Thy mercies, wast
pleased to bestow upon me the precious gift of a virtuous
wife, and in Thy good providence to entrust to our keeping most precious lambs of Thy flock, if it seem good in
Thy holy sight, let not these blessings in a day that is to
come rise up in judgment against me a poor worm of
the dust, but whilst prizing them highly as the gift of
Thy hand, enable me through them to look up to Thee
the great Giver, and to love Thee above all, who art in
Thyself the source of uncreated beauty, and of all that is
truly excellent! Thou only fully knowest how much my
weak heart is disposed to cling unto these Thy gifts,
and to be content therewith! But magnify Thy grace, I
beseech Thee, in redeeming my soul from too strong an
attachment to these things, and enable me to place my
affections more and more upon those things which are
above, and which never fade away! * * *

"8th mo. 14th, 1848.—Set out very early this morning, and had an interesting ride for twenty-one miles to
St. John's, on the outlet of Lake Champlain. Our road
lay through what is called the French settlement, which
extends a distance of several miles along a plank road
formed by the British government some years ago. The
land has been sold in lots of about fifty acres, and neat
log-houses and out-buildings have been erected on each
lot, presenting a valuable specimen of what might not
improperly be called 'the allotment system.' These cottages are built at the distance probably of one hundred
yards from each other, each of them having this frontage
to the road, and their land laying behind. The settlement extends for nearly ten miles on both sides of the
road, and the houses being whitewashed and in good

repair, present to the eye the appearance of comfort, which is truly gratifying, especially when we were told that twenty years ago this tract of land was nothing but one continued forest. The settlers are mostly French, and a few Irish. We reached St. John's about eleven o'clock, and took passage for ourselves and our horses on board a steamboat which left here at two o'clock for Whitehall, in the State of New York, at the upper end of the lake, a distance of one hundred and fifty miles, for which we paid ten dollars. The afternoon was very fine and agreeable, there being quite a breeze on the lake, which made it pleasant and refreshing to be on deck as long as we could, but on retiring to our berths for the night the heat was oppressive, so that little rest could be obtained, and in the morning of third day 15th, it was satisfactory to find ourselves very near Whitehall, and before six o'clock to be seated at breakfast at the Clinton Hotel, and about a quarter past that hour we were in our carriage and on the road to Sandy Hill, twenty-one miles distant, where we arrived before noon, and stayed to dine at a tavern. In the afternoon had a fatiguing journey of upwards of twenty miles on a heavy sandy road to Saratoga Springs, a place much frequented on account of its mineral waters. We found the town very full of company, but we met with pretty comfortable accommodation at Batch's Columbian Hotel, a house conducted on strictly temperance principles.

" Fourth day 16th.—This morning we took a ride to see the several springs of mineral waters in the neighbourhood, some of which are highly impregnated with different substances, which cannot fail to render them highly beneficial in many cases. We also fell in with several families of Indians encamped in a wood adjoining the town, the first time we had seen any of the aborigines since coming to this country. They appeared an interesting people. Two of the families were of the Oneidas, and the others of the St. Francis Indians from Canada.

They were employed in making baskets, bows and arrows, and other trinkets which they had for sale, and some of the boys were engaged shooting at a mark, at which they seemed moderately expert, some of them hitting a cent piece stuck in a log at the distance of several yards. About noon we had the satisfaction of receiving letters from home, which had been directed to meet us here, giving accounts of the welfare of our respective families, and in the afternoon we left Saratoga Springs, the most fashionable place of resort, we were told, in the United States, but very far short of many of our watering places in England in appearance, and came on fourteen miles to Bural Hill, where we met with comfortable accommodation for the night at a tavern.

" 8th mo. 18th, 1848.—As we are now within twenty-two miles of the Niagara Falls, we felt as if it might be allowable for us to go so far out of our way to see this great work of an Almighty Creator. We accordingly took our places in the railway cars which left Buffalo for the Falls at five in the evening, and had a pleasant ride along the Niagara River, and got there a little before sunset. We crossed the river below the Falls in a small boat rowed by two men, and had a pretty good view as we were on the water of the American Falls, but were not able this evening to get a good sight of the Horse Shoe Fall on the Canada side, which is much the larger of the two. We met with pretty comfortable accommodation at the Pavilion Hotel, about a mile and a half from the ferry, and next morning we were up about five o'clock, and soon made our way to the Table Rock, immediately below the Horse Shoe Fall, and down the spiral staircase, by which we descended to the bed of the river, and along a path on its margin to the very edge of the Great Fall, behind which there is a way by which some persons venture underneath the falling sheet of water, and which I suppose may be done with perfect safety, but as Benjamin and myself were quite alone and had made our way thus

far so as to have a very good view of this mighty cataract,
we did not feel disposed to venture any further, but con-
tented ourselves with wandering amongst the rocks on
the margin of the boiling flood, until it was time to return
to our inn to breakfast; after which we hired a carriage
to take us to the Suspension Bridge, a mile and a half
below the Falls, which crosses the river at the height of
two hundred and thirty feet above the water, and is eight
hundred feet in length.   We walked over it on paying a
toll of a quarter of a dollar, but it required great nerve to
venture to look down at the foaming waters beneath from
the giddy height at which we stood, especially when we
looked at the frailty of the bridge, and felt it tremble
under our feet at every step.   We then returned up the
American side to the Falls, crossed over to Goat Island,
and on to the Terapin Rocks, and to the top of the stone
tower erected there, from whence we had the best view of
the Horse Shoe Fall, and which is seen here in all its
sublimity and grandeur.   To see such a mighty mass of
water incessantly and steadily pouring over the precipice
into the abyss below is a scene which my pen would fail
to describe.   Suffice it to say that, although in common
with many others who visit the Falls, our first impression
was that of disappointment, yet the longer we viewed
them, the more the eye rested upon them, the greater,
the more magnificent, and the more sublime they appeared, so that on coming away I could not but say that
my expectations were realized.   On our return from Goat
Island we treated ourselves with a bathe in the pure
waters of Niagara, at an establishment erected for the
purpose on a small island called Bath Island, which is
situated in the midst of the Rapids, a short distance
above the Falls, and is connected with the mainland by
means of a wooden bridge.   After dining at the Falls
Hotel we left Niagara for Buffalo by the railroad cars,
much gratified with our visit, having been favoured with
beautiful weather, which added much to the pleasure of
surveying the scenery of the Falls.

" 25th 9 mo., 1848.—A day of rest at our comfortable quarters at our friend Elijah Coffins', which I have spent mostly in my chamber, and in writing to my dear wife and to my sister Martha Wright, of Kettering, and sweet it is to have an hour of quiet thus to commune with loved ones far away, to pour out the feelings and emotions of the heart into the bosom of those we love, as far as we are able to do it, through the medium of pen and ink, and although this falls infinitely short of personal intercourse, I feel it to be an inestimable privilege that this means of communication is afforded us when widely separated as to the outward from the dear objects of our affection, and I desire at this time to thank God for it."

After attending the opening of Indiana Yearly Meeting:—

" At four o'clock we attended a very interesting sitting of the African Committee, and at the close of that, the Committee on Education. By the reports brought up from the several quarters, it appears there are within the limits of this Yearly Meeting upwards of eight thousand of a suitable age to go to school, or between the ages of five and twenty-one, and of these nearly one half are instructed in schools under the care of Friends, the rest attend mixed or district schools."

Having attended the sittings of Indiana Yearly Meeting, B. S. and my father went to Cincinnatti, from whence they travelled to New Garden, in North Carolina, accompanied by a kind friend, to attend the Yearly Meeting there.

" In the afternoon we made twenty-six miles, and travelled some time after sunset in order to reach George's Tavern, which had been recommended to us as a desirable place for the night, but when we got there, although the landlord held two thousand acres of land, two hundred of which were under cultivation, and a number of slaves, yet we could procure no oats for our horses, nor anything they would eat. Indian corn was the only thing we could get for them, and the stable they were put into was little better than being out in the open air. And although only about forty miles from Cincinnatti, the 'Queen City of the West,' yet we understood that land in any quantity could be purchased for four or five dollars an acre, with a rich limestone soil, yielding from fifty to sixty bushels an acre; yet I suppose within the same distance from Cincinnatti, in the free State of Ohio, land of no better quality would fetch from sixty to eighty dollars. I am not aware, as far as I can learn, that this great difference in the value of land, and the different appearance of the country, is fairly to be attributed to anything but to the existence of slavery in the one state and freedom in the other. We, however, fared better than our horses, each of us being provided with a comfortable bed and a good supper.

"11th mo. 2nd, 1848.—* * * The weather is beautifully fine, with frosty nights and clear, bright, sunny days. Not a cloud to be seen in the sky. The foliage of the forest varied with almost every tint, but thickly falling from the trees, and showing already in many places the bare limbs. There is to me something of a melancholy, solemn pleasure in sauntering through the woods at such a season, treading the rustling leaves which have descended to their parent earth, and seeing those they have left for a short time on the stem on which they grew, severed from the branches by the rude touch of the coming winter, and in haste as it were to join their kindred dust. Emblems of the frailty of man! To-day he blooms; to-morrow he dies! * * *

"Baltimore, 12th mo. 15th.—This morning our friend Joseph King took us to see a coloured school, where

about a hundred and twenty of both sexes seem to be
receiving a good education in the common branches of
learning, under a competent teacher of their own colour.
They were nearly all free, the slaves being in general
debarred the privilege of learning to read. Before we
came away Benjamin addressed them in a feeling manner,
and we left them much pleased with our visit. When we
were in this city a year ago, we visited the establishment
of Hope Slatter, a noted slave dealer, who since that
time has given up the business to another individual,
having amassed a considerable fortune by the traffic in
the bones and sinews of his fellow-men. Whilst we were
in Richmond, in Virginia, a few weeks ago, we went to
visit another establishment of the same kind, belonging
to Bacon Tait of that city, another dealer in human flesh
and bones, but in every other respect a man of good
standing with his fellow-citizens, quite a gentleman in his
manners, and of good moral conduct. There we also met
with Hope Slatter, who was at that time residing in
Richmond, having purchased a beautiful residence, and
endeavouring to gain the respect and attention of the
citizens, so as to be admitted to their society. But it
appeared to be all in vain. Although slaveholders themselves, and feeling no objections to buy or sell slaves for
their own use and convenience, yet, strange as it may
seem, they stand aloof from the man who makes it his
business to traffic in them, and look down upon him as it
were with abhorrence. And we understood it is the case
throughout all the slave states. Although the slaveholders unhesitatingly deal with these traders when their
convenience requires it, yet will they not associate with
them, scarcely live in the same neighbourhood, nor even
allow them to worship with them at the same altar. This
is one of the anomalies in human nature which it is difficult to solve, at least for those who are not participators
in the system, and are disposed to consider the slave-
holder and the slave-dealer as standing on one common
platform.

"1st mo. 11th, 1849.—The way now seeming pretty clear to return towards Philadelphia, this morning we took leave of our kind friends at Bellefont, and took our places in the stage sleigh for Lewistown. The weather was very cold, the thermometer at sunrise being at zero. But being well wrapped up in our cloaks, and pretty closely packed (there being eight of us in the sleigh, which was a covered one), we did not suffer much inconvenience from it, but had a pleasant mountain journey of thirty miles to Lewistown, where we arrived about three in the afternoon; and, getting to a pretty comfortable inn, we concluded to stay here, instead of going on through the night, as we might have done; and accordingly we took our places in the stage which leaves at seven o'clock to-morrow morning for Scarrisburg, and this evening had a quiet opportunity for writing a little, which I much enjoyed.

"Sixth day, 12th.—Left Lewistown this morning in a covered sleigh drawn by four horses. Our road lay along the banks of the Juniata river, the scenery on which is very picturesque. We stopped to dine at Millerstown, and about fifteen miles above Harrisburg crossed the Susquehanna river on a wooden bridge half a mile in length, just at the point where it is joined by the Juniata. Our route after this down to Harrisburg was along its banks. In some places it is a mile or upwards in width, but it now presented little but the appearance of a solid mass of ice, the severe cold of the last day or two having congealed even this large body of water. We got to Harrisburg about six in the evening, and found comfortable quarters for the night at Buchler's Hotel, expecting to go on to-morrow morning to Philadelphia by the railroad cars which leave here at eight o'clock."

Whilst thus travelling about from place to place, my father's journal contains many allusions to the great trial and cross which he endured in the long-continued separation from his tenderly beloved wife, sometimes, he says, "almost more than nature can bear." But he knew to whom to look for strength in times of conflict and temptation, and many times had he to seek help from the Lord in seasons of distress and deep discouragement, ever feeling himself unworthy and incompetent for the service in which he was engaged. But after unburdening his heart to his heavenly Father, and pouring out his soul in prayer, he never failed to find his soul refreshed and his strength renewed, and he was able to go again on his way rejoicing.

"6th mo. 20th, 1849.—Left New Bedford this morning about eleven o'clock by the steamboat for the island of Nantucket. The distance is about sixty miles. The weather was beautifully fine, and the sea as smooth as a mill pond, so that we had a very favourable passage, reached our destination after a five hours' run, and were kindly received by our friend Cromwell Barnard and his wife, with whom we took up our quarters. We called on our way to land passengers at the small island of Nashaun, and at a larger one called Martha's Vineyard, and at a place on the main known by the name of Wood's Hole, near which is a narrow passage between the mainland and an island, where the sea runs at a rapid rate over a rocky bottom, causing a considerable eddy, so that it is considered dangerous for vessels of much size to go through it. Edward Gardner, a Friend of New Bedford, who was formerly captain of a whale ship, kindly accompanied us to Nantucket. At the entrance into the harbour we passed over a shoal a mile and a half in breadth, on which we were told there is not at high tide more than nine feet of water, so that a loaded ship cannot get in without taking out great part of her cargo, or being carried over the bar by what they call a 'camel,' a

D

recent contrivance, which appears to answer the purpose
very well, by which the vessel is buoyed up out of the
water, and carried over the shoal into the harbour, where
there is a good depth of water, and a secure berth from
all winds that usually blow here.

"The inhabitants of this island, which is about fifteen
miles long, and from three to four in width, are nearly
eight thousand in number, and are entirely dependent
on the whale fishery for a subsistence, the land here not
being of a nature to be cultivated to any advantage,
being very little else but barren sand. Friends here were
formerly very numerous, two Monthly Meetings being
kept up on the island; but now they are much reduced,
and scarcely able to keep up one. * * *

"Within the last few weeks I have had very much
before the view of my mind a prospect of religious service
in a *very* distant land, which has freshly and impressively
again and again been presented before me since landing
on these shores, accompanied with the renewed belief
that it will be required of me, when released from the
present field of labour on this continent, to stand resigned
to enter into as it may be pointed out by the great Head
of the Church. My mind has been introduced into deep
conflict in looking towards such a sacrifice being called
for at my hands who am truly the weakest and hinder-
most of the flock, and in no wise worthy to be employed
either to open or shut a door in the Lord's house. And
very bitter hath been the thought of being again called
upon to leave my nearest and dearest connections in life,
and go to the very uttermost parts of the earth. And
nothing less, I am persuaded, than the power of that
Almighty grace, to which all things are possible, can ever
bring my poor mind to a state of resignation to drink the
bitter cup. But if it is of the Lord, and the thing is
really from Him, I trust that He will enable me to bow
to His most holy will, and to take it at His hand as that
which He sees best for me, adopting according to my
small measure the language of our holy Exemplar: 'If

this cup may not pass from me except I drink it, not my will, oh Father, but Thine, be done.'

"7th mo. 2nd, New York.—The morning beautifully fine; the weather not so hot as some days past. Took a walk down to the Battery to have a view of the harbour and shipping, a fine and interesting sight. Father Matthew, from Ireland, the apostle of Temperance, arrived on sixth day last, and is expected to be escorted into New York this afternoon. He has been staying since his arrival on Staten Island, a few miles below the city. He appears to meet with a very cordial reception in this country, and I trust his influence may have a beneficial effect in promoting the cause in which he has been so successfully engaged in his native land. * * *

"Being informed that there was a settlement of Indians on our way betwixt Collins and Ellery, we set out this afternoon about three o'clock, accompanied by our kind host and his wife, and two other friends, and rode through 'the Reservation' which is still secured to this injured people. It is a tract of land on the Cattarnugers Creek, about ten miles square. They have cleared several patches of it, and have some in good cultivation. A few of them have very good frame houses and barns, and appear to be doing well. One upon whom we called said he had seventeen acres this year in wheat, besides several acres in corn. The Hicksites have a school on the Reservation, under the charge of a family from Pennsylvania, where between twenty and thirty girls are boarded, clothed, and educated, and seem to be under good management. On the whole we were much pleased with what we saw amongst them, and thought them advancing fast in the arts of civilization. They are of the Seneca nation of Indians, and their number on this Reservation we understood to be six or seven hundred. We noticed some amongst them as white as most Europeans, and who, but for their Indian countenances, we should not have thought to belong to this people. After spending two or three hours amongst them, we went on to the Friend's house where we expected to lodge, and arrived there soon after sunset.

"2nd 8 mo.—This morning early we left our friend Ambrose Haights, where we lodged last night, and had an interesting day's journey of forty-one miles to Ellery, where there are three or four families of Friends settled at a considerable distance from any other Meeting. They have no meeting house, but they keep up a Meeting on first and fifth days, assembling in one of their dwelling-houses for the purpose. Arrangements were made this evening for our having a meeting with them at eleven o'clock to-morrow morning. Our journey to-day was through a fine tract of country on the south shore of Lake Erie. The roads were good, and the houses of the settlers seemed comfortable, and their general appearance thriving. We stopped for dinner at a pleasant village called Fredonia, which had the marks of being a place of considerable trade. The house of our Friend Levi Hoag, where we are lodging, is in sight of the Chatangua Lake, a sheet of water about twenty miles in length, and from half a mile to two and a half in breadth. It is at an elevation of several hundred feet above Lake Erie, though probably not more than ten miles from it. Its outlet is into the Alleghany river, which runs towards the south.

"9th mo. 12th.—Left Mahoningtown about seven, and had a fine morning's ride through a thinly settled country, passing through Newcastle and Mercer on our way, and at noon stopped at a small country tavern to dine, where they told us they had a call from the President about two weeks ago, who has recently been making a tour through several of the States. We understood he travelled without any state or equipage, being only accompanied by a son-in-law and a few gentlemen from the last place where he had been stopping. The landlady said he had the appearance and manners of a plain country farmer."

B. S. and my father had been presented with a carriage
and pair of horses after their arrival in America by some
kind Friends, and their usual mode of travelling was in
this carriage.

"9th mo. 15th.—This morning it was satisfactory to
find that our lame horse was much better, so that we
journeyed on pretty comfortably, though the weather was
oppressively warm and the roads very dusty, and it was
truly pleasant when, after a fatiguing travel of six days,
we stopped this evening a little before sunset at the door
of our friend Samuel Carey, at Buffalo, and received a
kind welcome to his house, though sorry to find his wife
sick in bed, but not, we hope, seriously ill. We have
travelled 256 miles from Mount Pleasant, Ohio, to this
place, within the last six days, which, considering the
rough country we have had to pass over, has been pretty
severe upon our horses: but hope, with a little rest, they
will soon be recruited. They are a pair of valuable
animals, gentle and tractable, and always ready for their
work.

"Second day, 17th.—* * * We left Buffalo on our
way to Pelham, crossing the ferry at Black Rock, where
we parted with our worthy friend Samuel Carey, and once
more set our feet on the British Dominions, though in a
foreign land. On enquiring our best way to Pelham of
the Custom-house officer on the Canada side of the river,
we were informed it would be by 'the Falls,' of which we
were not aware before; but hearing this, and on referring
to the account of Meetings finding that the Select Quarterly Meeting of Pelham did not begin until two o'clock
to-morrow afternoon, we pretty soon concluded to bend
our course that way, and to stay all night at the Falls,
and go on to Pelham in the morning, which we found we
could easily do, it being only twelve miles distant. And
I believe we have had no reason to regret having come to

this conclusion, as we found the road very good, and had a most beautiful and interesting drive of eighteen miles on the banks of the Niagara river down to the Falls, where we arrived soon after four o'clock, and put up at the Clifton House, a large and well-conducted hotel immediately in full view of the Falls on the Canada side.

"After enjoying an evening's view of these wonderful works of our great Creator, we retired to our room for the night, having the music of their roar to hush our wandering thoughts, and draw our minds to solemn contemplation. At the Clifton House we found Lord Elgin, the Governor-General of the Canadas, and his suite. We understood he had been there for a fortnight past, but was now about going away. We occupied a lodging room which some of his party left this evening.

"9th mo. 18th.—We were both up very early this morning. Before breakfast I took a walk to the Suspension Bridge, a mile and a half below the Falls, and had the fearful pleasure of walking back and forth over the dizzy height for the payment of a quarter of a dollar; and on my return to the inn, I found Benjamin sitting on the upper piazza, from whence he had enjoyed a beautiful sunrise, and seen its effects in producing all the colours of the rainbow on the cloud of mist and spray continually arising from the larger, or Horse Shoe, Fall on the Canada side. After breakfast, and again enjoying for a while a full view of this stupendous work of nature, we took our leave of the Falls, and bent our course eastward through an interesting part of the country to Pelham, where we arrived about noon, and took dinner at our friend Samuel Taylor's, near the meeting house.

"25th.—* * * This evening I much enjoyed a quiet walk in the adjoining wood, where, sitting on a log, or strolling beneath the shade of the sugar maple, I watched the rays of the setting sun gild the tops of the trees before he sunk to rest beneath the western horizon, and

thought of those near and dear to me in a far distant
land.

"28th.—Left Toronto this morning at half-past seven
in the steamboat called the 'Chief Justice,' and had a
tossing voyage of three hours across the lake to Lewiston,
from whence we came on to Buffalo by railroad, and
reached our friend Samuel Carey's soon after four, where
we stayed tea, and in the evening went on board the
steamer for Sandusky, expecting to sail about nine
o'clock; but, from some cause or other, the vessel did
not start at the time appointed, and we were obliged to
retire to our berths in uncertainty as to the hour we
should leave, which was very trying, as our time to reach
our destination before the commencement of Indiana
Yearly Meeting was very limited, and how increasingly
so was it on the morning of

"Seventh day, 29th, to find ourselves still in port, and
unable to find out whether we should sail in the course of
the day. It is indeed a trial of patience, as well as a
proving of faith, inducing us to look back and trace our
steppings thus far in the present movement, more particularly as all hope of reaching Indiana in time for the
opening of the Yearly Meeting appears, from this detention, to be at an end.
"And in this search it is cause of thankfulness humbly
to believe that it has been our endeavour simply to follow
the pointings of the Divine Finger as far as we have been
enabled to see them; and under this feeling the desire is
raised to leave all these things over which we have no
control to the ordering of Him whose ways are not as our
ways, and who is able out of seeming evil still to educe
good.
"About ten in the forenoon we had the satisfaction to
see the captain give orders to move the vessel; and by
eleven we were fairly out of the harbour and on our way;
and although there was some wind, yet not so much as

to raise a sea, and the boat being also a steady one, we got on very favourably without any sickness, which was more than I expected from what we had seen the previous morning in crossing Lake Ontario. We made good progress throughout the day, and on the morning of

"First day, the 30th, we entered Sandusky Bay, having made the distance of 265 miles in nineteen hours, including a stoppage of an hour and a half at Cleveland to land and receive passengers. We were also pleased to find that arrangements had been made for a train to leave Sandusky at eight o'clock this morning, in order to take passengers forward to Springfield and Cincinnatti, so that we had only just time to get breakfast before we were in the cars on our way to Springfield in Ohio. The day was wet, but we were favoured to get on without accident, and by five in the evening reached our destination for the night. After getting our supper, and taking our places in the stage for Richmond, which passes here at four o'clock in the morning, we retired to bed to get some rest, of which we felt a good deal in need, not having had our clothes off for the last two nights. We met with indifferent accommodation at the Murray House in Springfield; but for this, I trust, we were desirous to be thankful to our great and bountiful Provider and Caretaker, whose comforting and consoling presence has been mercifully near during the fatigues and trials of the last three or four days in an especial manner, which favour I desire at this time gratefully to commemorate, and to acknowledge that 'the Lord hath helped hitherto.'

"Second day, 10th mo. 1st.—This morning left Springfield by the public stage very early, and had a long and tedious day's journey in travelling 64 miles, only reaching our friend Elijah Coffin's at Richmond a little before sunset. Here we had the comfort of meeting with several other dear Friends, who, like ourselves, were come to attend the ensuing Yearly Meeting. We had also the

satisfaction to learn that the first sitting of the Meeting
for Sufferings, as well as the Select Yearly Meeting, are
held to-morrow; so that, after all our delays and little
perplexities in getting along, we find we are in full time
for the business of the Yearly Meeting. And thus hath
the Lord in His goodness caused all to work together for
good, and brought us safely and in due time to our desired
haven thus far.

"What a lesson hath this journey afforded us to trust
in Him at all times, and endeavour in simple and un-
questioning faith to commit our way unto the Lord, even
when we may not be able to understand the why and the
wherefore of some things which He sees meet to permit,
and which at the time may seem to be against us, most
assuredly believing that He will do all things both well
and wisely! We have travelled upwards of five hundred
miles since leaving Toronto in Upper Canada on sixth
day morning last, so that it is very pleasant to have
reached a resting place after a long, fatiguing, and in
some respects harassing, yet interesting journey. The
weather is much cooler than it was a week ago, and the
country in passing along has quite an autumnal appearance, the foliage of some of the forest trees being already
beautifully varied in their hues from the sombre brown to
the brightest scarlet.

"Kingston, 10th mo. 26th.— * * * Whilst riding
along this morning from Adolphustown to this place, with
my mind turned inward to the Lord, He was pleased very
clearly to bring to my view a prospect, which hath before
been presented to my mind, of the place where I must be
willing to spend the evening of my days, when the more
active service in distant fields of labour, which must be
entered upon in their season, shall be accomplished. The
prospect of this requiring was bitter as gall and wormwood to my taste, inasmuch as my nature clings to the
home of my youth; and, in my wanderings in this land,
my mind hath often turned with pleasure and with hope

to the thought of spending my declining years in the home of my fathers, which, in a way that I once looked not for, the Lord has been pleased to give into my possession. But I can thankfully acknowledge that as I endeavoured to dwell under this prospect, a degree of holy resignation was vouchsafed, and I was enabled to bow to His behest, and cheerfully to take the bitter cup, and to say in mine heart, ' Not my will, oh Father, but Thine, be done.'

" 10th mo. 27th.—This morning at seven o'clock we left Kingston by the mail steamer down the River St. Lawrence, and had a most interesting voyage of sixty miles to Brocksville, a flourishing and improving place on the western bank of that river. On our way we passed that part known by the name of ' the Thousand Islands,' and had a most beautiful sail amongst them. We were told that their number considerably exceeds a thousand, and I can readily believe it, as the river for a distance of upwards of forty miles is thickly studded with them, and its width varies in that distance from four or six to eight or ten miles. They are of all sizes, from a few yards across to a mile in length, and some much larger. They are mostly rocky islands, but covered with trees and shrubs of different kinds, the foliage of which, at this season of the year, was of every hue, and had a most striking and beautiful appearance. Some of the larger islands are inhabited, and bear the marks of good cultivation.

" 2nd 1st mo., 1850.—This morning we found the snow deeper, and worse travelling for our horses. We, however, reached Pigeon, a village on the edge of a large prairie, in good dinner time, where we stopped and fed our horses. Here we left the main road which runs across the State from Detroit to Chicago, and found the roads worse, which made it very tedious getting along. so that it was eight o'clock in the evening when we arrived at our friend Isaac Bonine's, of Prairie Grove.

The whole distance we made to-day was only thirty-eight miles, and I do not remember a more tedious day's journey for a long time owing to the snow; but I think it is probable before we leave here we shall change our wheels for runners, which will make it much easier for our horses as well as pleasanter for ourselves. The country through which we passed to-day was thinly settled, and the land, with the exception of the prairies, was only very indifferent. The Pigeon Prairie is from eight to ten miles square, but Young's, upon which our friend Isaac Bonine is located, is only from two to three miles across. The soil is a rich black earth of a good depth, which produces large crops, particularly of Indian corn. There is no timber upon them, and for the most part they present one flat unbroken surface, though some, we understand, are a little rolling.

"1st mo. 10th.—* * * Our route lay at a short distance from Lake Michigan; the land thinly wooded, with openings of marsh or prairie, on which we saw two wild deer feeding not far from us, but on being disturbed they quickly bounded off, and were soon out of sight. They were the first we have fairly got a sight of in all our journeyings on this continent, though we have often looked out for them in passing through the forests, and have felt disappointed at not seeing them. Whilst waiting for our dinners where we stopped at noon, we were called out by one of our party to see the distant prairie on fire. The flames appeared to extend as much as a mile in width, and to make rapid progress in the direction of the wind, sending forth a dense volume of smoke. The fire moved away from us, so that we soon lost sight of it. We understood it is not uncommon to set fire to the long dried grass at this season of the year, though it is sometimes attended with disastrous consequences to persons travelling across the wide prairies, and some lives have been lost by it. Before sunset we reached Chicago, in the State of Illinois, one of the many mushroom cities of the West, which have sprung up within the last twenty years. Chicago is situated on the western side of Lake Michigan, and already contains nearly thirty thousand inhabitants, and is a place of considerable trade, having ready communication, by steamers which ply on the lake, with all the eastern cities. Great quantities of produce are shipped from here every season. Pork, one of the principal articles of export, is at present very low. We have heard of its being sold at Chicago this winter at a dollar and a half per hundred. But although provisions are so cheap, we have not yet found the charges at the taverns to be much lower than in the older settled parts, though we are told that we shall find this to be the case as we proceed further westward. Our expenses hitherto have generally been about four dollars a day for ourselves and our horses.

" 19th.—We reached the Mississippi River this morning about eleven o'clock, and on enquiry it appeared as if it might be safe to cross over on the ice, though there had been some accidents very recently from parties attempting it—one of a very serious character forty miles down the river, when a carriage containing six individuals broke through, and instantly disappeared under the ice, and four of them perished. In order to lighten our carriage we got out and walked over, whilst the ferryman drove our horses across on the ice, and I am thankful to say that we all reached the other side in safety.

"1st mo. 23rd.—East Grove.— * * * After leaving here we pretty soon entered upon a prairie nearly twenty miles over, without a single house or inhabitant upon it. About sunset we had got more than half way across, when we came to a creek three or four feet deep and probably twenty yards wide, the ice on which was partly thawed, so as not to bear the weight of our horses, and yet so strong that we could not break our way through it, so that we were under the necessity of going back to the last house we had passed, which was at least ten miles distant, and ask for a night's lodging. We reached it about eight o'clock, but the owner of it said he could not accommodate us, but directed us to another house two or three miles further. A second time we were disappointed, but on our third application we succeeded in getting a shelter for ourselves and our horses. Benjamin and myself were privileged with a bed, but our friends who were with us had to lie on the floor, covered with their buffalo robes; but although it was only a mean place, and the man charged us a dollar and a half for our accommodation, without furnishing us with anything more than some feed for our horses, yet we had cause to be thankful for it, as the night proved very stormy and wet."

B. S. and my father were at this time travelling through the State of Ohio, and during their journey of four hundred miles from Michigan, which occupied them thirteen days, going in their own carriage, and putting up at some tavern for the night, they had not met with a single Friend, or any in profession with them. After crossing the Des Moines River, they appeared to have reached the verge of civilization westward, about a dozen miles further being the last village of any size settled by the whites, the Indians having occupied this part of the country only four years ago; but having sold out their rights to the United States, they were located beyond the Missouri River. The prairie wolves were noticed for the first time, which are rather smaller than the common wolf, and are very destructive to the sheep and lambs of the settlers. Here were found small settlements of Friends, and in some places meetings were established, in others the meeting was held in a log cabin or schoolhouse. As the time was winter, my father suffered much from the cold, the log houses allowing the wind a great deal of access. One night, although a good fire was kept up, the thermometer in the morning stood at 20° below zero. As a specimen of one of their places of accommodation, my father's journal says :—

"2nd mo. 4th.—At the house where we lodged last night, and which was only a single room, about 18 feet by 16 feet, twelve individuals were accommodated. Our company, consisting of four men, were privileged to occupy the two beds, and the family, consisting of the Friend, his wife, and four children, and a young man who was also there, were arranged on the floor and on a trundle bedstead which was drawn out from beneath one of the other beds. There was a good fire most of the night, and the openings between the logs of which the building was composed being well plastered up with mud, we were more comfortable and warm that we had been for several nights past; and I may say, that under this humble roof we were treated with genuine hospitality, and I do not remember to have felt myself more at home for a long time."

After completing the visit to Friends in Iowa, our travellers set out for a settlement in the east of the State of Illinois, a distance of about three hundred miles, and which took nine or ten days to accomplish, as the roads were very bad and dangerous, being often nothing but cross logs, or what was called "corduroy;" and often encountering deep sloughs in crossing the prairies, it was thought best that a Friend should accompany them. In endeavouring to cross one of the sloughs, in which were two or three feet of water, the horses stuck fast, and fell down; and after two hours' labour, and the help of four men and a yoke of oxen, they were able to extricate the carriage, which had sustained but little damage, and to continue their journey. Sometimes it seemed as if the carriage would be jolted to pieces, and it was no easy matter to bear the continual shaking which the bad roads occasioned.

My father observed in the woods many very large trees. One oak tree he had the curiosity to measure, and at 3 feet from the ground its circumference was 22 feet, and at 6 feet from the earth it measured 20 feet round, keeping the same size to the height of thirty or forty feet. At Spiceland, the Friend at whose house they lodged had two large poplar trees cut down in the wood. Their height was about 130 feet, and 4 feet in diameter. My father says: "It was truly a fine sight to see them fall. The sound echoed through the forest like distant thunder, and the ground trembled with the shock to the distance of two or three hundred yards from where they fell."

"7th mo. 22nd, 1850.—* * * On our way we made a call, and spent four or five hours with feelings of much interest at the Shakers' establishment, four miles from Lebanon, in Warren county, Ohio. We were very kindly received, and shown over the institution; and their arrangements and manner of living were fully explained to us, and we could not but exceedingly admire the cleanliness, neatness, order, and regularity which was manifest throughout. They own about six square miles of very fine land, and only a small part of it is under cultivation. Their whole number of men, women, and children, we understood, was from five to six hundred, and these are divided into five large families, located on different parts of the estate. Each family is under the superintendence of elders of both sexes, though all unite together for general purposes. They have manufactories of various kinds amongst them, and give evidence of being a very industrious people. Although both men and women live in the same buildings, yet they have separate apartments for the sexes, and do not allow of any connection between them further than as brethren and sisters. We dined with them, and were treated with genuine hospitality, and felt great freedom in asking any questions respecting their particular tenets, which they as freely answered; but it was great cause of regret to find that their views were decidedly Unitarian. They have several other establishments of the same kind in different parts of the United States, which they suppose may altogether contain about four thousand individuals. They bear the character of being a moral, orderly people. We found several amongst them who had been brought up as members of our Society. One, an interesting young woman named Persis Hoag, cousin to our valued friend L. M. Hoag, who has been in the establishment four years, and appears to be highly esteemed amongst them.

"New Bedford, Massachusetts, 4th mo. 1st, 1851.— Resting to-day at our friend George Howlands'. Took a walk down into the town this morning, and noticed great activity amongst the shipping; some busy unloading, and others preparing to depart. No less than three hundred vessels belong to this port, employed almost exclusively in whaling, and the last season has been a very successful one, rapidly enriching those engaged in it. Our worthy host has had one just returned from a voyage of twenty months, with a cargo of 2,800 barrels of oil, which will probably realize him a net profit of upwards of twenty thousand dollars, or four thousand pounds sterling. Another vessel, belonging to some other party, had just discharged her cargo of 3,500 barrels, and would most likely yield a clear profit to the owner of six thousand pounds sterling. Most of the ships engaged in the business have done well the past year, though some seasons they 'toil long and take but little.' But on the whole it

appears to have been a profitable business for some years
past to those who are embarked in it. In my walk this
afternoon I saw another vessel which had been in port a
few days after being out thirty months, and had taken
5,000 barrels of oil and 75,000 pounds of bone, the value
of which at the present prices was about ninety thousand
dollars, which, after deducting the expenses of outfit and
wages, would probably leave a surplus of forty thousand.
The crew of a whale ship, according to the general practice of the trade in these parts, receive about one-third of
the value of the cargo as their share, being virtually
partners to a certain extent. Our friend George Howland
and two of his sons who are in partnership with him
have eight ships engaged in the whaling business.

"7th mo. 7th, 1851.—It is four years and eight months
this morning since we landed at Boston, and I have been
down there this afternoon in company with my kind
friend Stephen A. Chase, to put our baggage on board
the steamer 'Europa,' now lying in Boston harbour, with
the expectation of sailing on fourth day for Liverpool.
When I look back at the time we have spent here, the
extent of the country over which we have travelled, the
dangers we have passed through, the perils we have been
in, both seen and unseen, and remember that no harm
has been permitted to befall us either by night or by day,
'through burning climes have passed unhurt, and breathed
in tainted air,' even in places where the pestilence was
walking in darkness, and the angel of death was fulfilling
his dread commission; when I consider that through all
this we have been favoured with uninterrupted health,
and have never been prevented by the want of it from
travelling or attending meetings, even for a single day;
when I consider these things, I am constrained to
acknowledge that nothing short of the Lord's all-pow-
erful arm could have preserved us, and to Him do I
desire to return thanks for this marvellous display of
His goodness to us poor unworthy creatures, to whom

E

belongeth nothing but blushing and confusion of face,
but to Him, the Lord our God, all the praise. * * *
During this period we have travelled on the American
continent by land and by water 32,373 miles, two-thirds
at least of that distance in our own private conveyance,
kindly furnished us soon after our arrival in America
by our Philadelphia Friends, and with the same horses.
The rest of the distance at various times as it seemed
convenient, was performed by steamboat, railroad cars,
public stage, and occasionally letting our horses rest
a while, and accepting the kind assistance of our friends
from one meeting to another in their conveyances. We
have attended in that time 966 Meetings for Worship,
117 Monthly Meetings, 55 Quarterly Meetings, and the
various services of 22 Yearly Meetings, viz., four times at
Ohio, Philadelphia, New York, and New England; thrice
at Indiana; twice at North Carolina, and once at Baltimore Yearly Meeting, besides attending many select
Preparative and Quarterly Meetings, and various other
services in public and in private, both in families and with
individuals. * * * We visited all parts of the American
continent where there are meetings, and, with the exception of a few small ones in Philadelphia and New
England Yearly Meetings, were at nearly all the settled
meetings of Friends in America. In the course of this
extensive visit, we have travelled pretty thoroughly
through twenty of the States. * * * This afternoon we
took a ride, in company with several other Friends, down
to Nahant, a small promontory jutting out into the sea
three or four miles, and connected with the mainland by
a narrow beach, which is sometimes covered by the water.
Nahant is frequented as a bathing place and as a summer
resort of the Boston people. The extremity of the land
presents a face of sharp precipitous rocks, threatening
certain destruction to any unfortunate vessel which may
be driven upon them. On our return, we called to look
through the garden and grounds of an individual of the
name of Tudor, who has amassed a considerable fortune

as an ice merchant, being the first person who conceived the idea of making it an article of commerce with foreign nations. We understood he has now several vessels employed in the trade, and exports large quantities to the East and West Indies."

After a favourable voyage of eleven days, my father and B. Seebohm reached Liverpool—

" When a small steamer soon came to us to land the mails and passengers, by which some of our Liverpool Friends reached us with a cordial welcome to our native shores, among the first of whom was my eldest son Thomas, who had been waiting my arrival since yesterday, and whom it was truly pleasant to see."

Of a little meeting held in their state room during the voyage, my father says :

" And though our meeting was altogether silent, yet it was a remarkably solemn season, and one which I believe will not be forgotten by me, from the clear and renewed revival of a concern which has been weightily brought before my mind at different times within the last five years, to visit in gospel love some very distant lands, and the isles afar off, with the evidence sealed upon my mind at this time that it was indeed the Lord's requiring, and that the time was not far distant when I must be resigned to give up to it. My very soul was prostrated into the dust under the sense of it ; and the cup felt exceedingly bitter, like unto wormwood and gall ; yet durst I not shut mine ears or mine eyes to the vision, but trust there was in mine heart a prayer raised to be enabled truly to say, ' If this cup may not pass away from me, except I drink it, Thy will be done.' "

As the " Europa " arrived at Liverpool about noon on the Sunday, their luggage could not be passed through

the Custom-house till the next day, and my father was
obliged to remain all night, and on Monday

"Left for Brighouse, and after a pleasant and agreeable journey were favoured to reach there about five
o'clock, and to find my dear family all well. It would be
difficult to describe the feelings of my mind on approaching my home, from which I had been so long separated,
and I may thankfully acknowledge that my mind was preserved in a very quiet state, not the least excitement
being permitted to prevail to disturb the peaceful serenity
with which I was favoured to look forward to meeting
again my dear wife and children. I found them all well,
my wife and four daughters who were at home with their
mother; and on sitting down to tea with them, and
seeing them all around me, and the evidence which was
afforded to my mind that during my long absence they
had in an especial manner been under the care of One
who had cared for them in every sense, my joy seemed
full, and I thought there could not possibly arrive to me
here upon earth an hour of more unmixed happiness."

After a truly happy week spent at home, surrounded by
his beloved family, and in renewed intercourse with his
dear friends, which he highly appreciated, after being so
long deprived of their society, he went to Kettering to see
his two sisters, Martha Wright and Esther Lindsey; and
from thence, accompanied by his brother-in-law, Francis
Ellington Wright, and his two sons, went to London to
see the Industrial Exhibition held in the Crystal Palace,
Hyde Park, and visited several other places of interest in
the city. After returning home, he had a desire to see
his native place, Gildersome. So, accompanied by his
wife and daughters, he spent a day there, calling upon
some of his old friends, who remembered the family. The

village he found in rather a decaying state, and the meeting of Friends there very small.

"Brighouse, 4th day, 10th mo. 1st, 1851.—Our week-day meeting this morning was a season of deep exercise to my mind, a prospect of service in a far-distant land being afresh brought livingly to my mind, with the belief that the time draws on apace when resignation on my part must be yielded to the Divine requiring, if peace be my portion; and, bitter as the cup is in prospect, a humble hope has been raised in my heart that the Lord will strengthen me to lay the sacrifice on His holy altar whether it may have to be offered up or not. For the service, and the undertaking altogether, seem to be of that magnitude and importance that I can scarcely believe my Friends will be willing to liberate me for it; but the Lord's will be done, and not mine, is my sincere prayer respecting it. I am now closely engaged, and have been for the last three weeks, in making some alterations in our premises for the more comfortable accommodation of my family, and in the doing of which I have great pleasure and satisfaction; though it may be that almost as soon as they are done, and I have made my little homestead all that I could desire, I may have speedily to leave it, and again become a wanderer in a foreign land." * * *

AUSTRALIAN JOURNEY.

IN the 7th mo. 1852 our dear father sailed for Hobart Town, with Frederic Mackie as companion, to prosecute the religious labours to which he believed himself called in the Australian colonies. Many Friends accompanied them to the ship, and prayers were put up for their preservation and guidance. The parting again from our beloved mother was a trying and heart-rending season, and from all his near and dear relatives and friends. My father suffered much from sea-sickness, and was often unable to be in any but a recumbent position even on deck. The ship they were in was a sailing vessel, so that when the wind was not in the right direction, their progress was very slow and tedious.

"7th day, 31st.—Becalmed off Cape St. Vincent. The wind had been falling during the night, and this morning it died away, so that now, at noon, we are laying idly on the waters, our sails, which are mostly unfurled, lazily flapping against the yards, scarcely indicating which way the current of air is moving. The ocean, which a few days ago was lashed with the stormy wind, scarcely shows a ruffle on its glassy surface. The human frame is languid and dull, and longs for the returning breeze. For my own part, I feel it affect me a good deal, but trust that patience may be granted to bear all the trials which may be permitted to attend this watery pilgrimage, undertaken, as I humbly trust it was, not in mine own will, but in the will of Him who hath a right to dispose of His dependent creatures as seemeth Him good. Temperature

in my cabin 73°. The colour of the ocean in this calm
is most beautiful, a lovely submarine tinge of its deep
waters making the jelly fish and pretty nautilus with its
wide-spread sail visible to our sight. Very few fish of
any kind to be seen in these parts, and none of the
feathered fowl that inhabit its bosom, except the stormy
petrel or Mother Carey's chickens, have favoured us with
their company. * * * A fine turtle swam close past the
ship, which some of us would have been glad to have
taken in order to make a change of food, but he was
quickly out of our reach. A little pilot fish was also seen
for some hours under our bows, giving us some reason to
think that a shark might be at no great distance, but
although a pretty sharp look-out has been kept up, he has
not yet been seen. * * *

"Another fine morning with a fair wind carrying us
on at about six knots an hour. Our fresh water is still
very good, and we can have as much as we need, including a little for washing; but since reaching the tropics,
everything has become so warm, and our water amongst
the rest, that it has become sickly to the taste, and one
is obliged to have it flavoured with something in order to
make it at all palatable, and in this way I have found our
lemon juice and raspberry vinegar very useful. * * *

"On second day morning when almost becalmed, a
young shark was observed following in the wake of our
vessel, and a line being put out baited with a piece of
pork, we soon had the pleasure of seeing him hauled up
on deck. Although not more than four feet in length,
his strength appeared to be very great, and until secured
by the sailors it was dangerous to come within his reach,
as I suppose a stroke from his tail while flouncing about
on deck would have been in danger of breaking a man's
leg. The sailors soon despatched him with their knives,
and had him dressed for the cook. The meat we understood was firm and solid but not very tender, and
considered tolerably palatable by some of the steerage
passengers who were privileged to partake of it. A

much larger one was seen by the second mate alongside early in the day, which seized a wooden block that
accidentally fell overboard and swallowed it in an instant,
but he was not afterwards to be seen. A day or two
ago, one of our crew reported one having passed our
stern of a very large size, he thought as much as from
twenty to thirty feet in length. A shoal of black fish,
a species of the whale, was also seen to windward spout-
ing and flouncing about, enjoying the storm which we
were suffering from. * * *

" Although so near the equator, the weather is cooler
and more pleasant than it was a fortnight ago, which is
a great favour. We passed to the south of the sun a
week ago, and have now to look to the north instead of
the south to see him at noonday, which seems strange to
us. The temperature of our cabin has been upwards of
80° for two or three weeks, which would be peculiarly
trying if we could not have our scuttles open through
the night, which we have been able to have with very
little exception ever since we have been out. My clothing through the day is one of my light striped shirts, a
pair of linen trousers, and an open coat, which I find
quite as much as I can bear.

" A Dutch schooner, which had been in sight for two
or three days, was this morning sailing for two or three
hours almost within a stone's throw of us. Being bound
to Pernambuco, on the coast of South America, some
of our passengers at the breakfast table suggested our
sending letters by her, to be forwarded from thence to
England, which our captain kindly assenting to, some of
our company were quickly engaged in writing, and in
about half an hour nearly twenty letters were delivered
to our first mate, who put off in one of our boats for the
schooner, which was then about a quarter of a mile distant, having laid-to on our making known our desire of
boarding them. Two or three of our passengers assisted
in rowing, which was no easy work, there being rather a
heavy swell, although a comparatively calm sea. Frederic

and myself each sent a few lines to our connections, informing them of our welfare and of our whereabouts, which no doubt will be grateful information to them. I had previously written a few lines addressed to my dear wife, in readiness for such an opportunity, which I also enclosed, but did not think it desirable to forward my journal at this time, thinking it rather an uncertain channel of conveyance, but unwilling to omit it altogether. * *

"I have just opened a note from my daughter Hannah, directed 'to be opened under the Equator,' and feel it truly grateful to refer to this memento of affectionate remembrance from my dear girl, bringing very vividly before the view of my mind the different members of my beloved family. * * * My thoughts within these few days have been very much with those dear ones whom I have left far behind, the remembrance of whom comes across my mind at seasons in such a way as almost to unman me, feeling it almost more than I can bear to think that I am so far from them, and that in all probability years must elapse before we are again restored to each other. * *

"During the past night I had a pleasant dream of being in the company of my dear wife. The interview was short, and I do not remember that any words passed on either side, but the look and expression of my dear partner's countenance was such as I desire not soon to forget. It was very serious, but tranquil, resigned, and heavenly. I am not in the way of taking much, if any, notice of dreams in general, yet there are some which leave such an unction behind them that we cannot doubt the source from whence they spring, and this I count one of the few such with which I have been favoured during my pilgrimage through this vale of tears. My mind for some time past has been much drawn towards home, and my beloved wife in particular, in such a way as to make me at times anxious and uneasy respecting them; but the sight of my beloved wife with which I was favoured last night, has had a very strengthening and settling effect, as if she had said to me, 'Thou seest, my dear, although

my burdens in thy absence are many, and my trials not a
few, the Lord is near, and gives me strength equal to the
day. Be thou also, my beloved husband, faithful in following the leadings of His Spirit, and thou also will be
favoured to know Him to strengthen thee for the work of
thy day, and in the end crown thee with the reward of
peace.' * *

" A few days ago we were much amused in viewing the
gambols of a monster of the deep (supposed by our captain
to be a grampus) throwing himself entirely out of the
water, and falling back again upon his side or his back
with a tremendous splash. We judged his length to be
from twenty to thirty feet. * *

" The ocean the last two days has presented a magnificent spectacle, the tops of the high curling billows flying
before the breeze like driven snow. The maindeck of our
vessel, from the breaking waves, has been flooded great
part of the day, making us feel the privilege of a dry poop
for needful exercise.

" For the last four or five weeks, since I got over my
sea-sickness, I think I have enjoyed as good health as at
any time of my life. When the weather is at all suitable,
I generally walk on deck three or four hours every day ;
and when it is too rough to walk, get hold of the ropes,
and exercise by jumping up and down, all which I find to
be needful and useful for the sake of health ; and by this
means, through mercy, I feel as well as I usually do on
shore, and am recovering my flesh, which I lost in the
early part of the voyage. * *

" The last night was very squally, and the wind rather
against us, and we got driven so far to the southward
that it was noon to-day before we got sight of the
Newstone, a high pyramidal rock on the coast of Van
Dieman's Land, soon after which we saw the mainland,
and are now off Whale Head, a lofty, bold promontory,
and making for Storm Bay, into which our captain hopes
to run this evening, though it is not likely that we can
get into the Derwent with the present wind.

"11th mo. 10th, 1852.—Last evening, about sunset, we rounded Tasman's Head, and entered Storm Bay; but the wind being from the northward prevented our making much progress. Our captain tacked through the night, and about eight in the morning we got a pilot on board, and worked up pretty much against the wind until we entered the river Derwent, when, the wind turning rather more in our favour, we got to an anchor off the town about four in the afternoon. A number of boats came off with parties to meet their friends, and, amongst the rest, George Washington Walker and Joseph Benson Mather kindly came on board, and welcomed us amongst them. * * * Thus, after a remarkably pleasant voyage of one hundred and ten days from the Downs, and being just sixteen weeks on board, were we permitted once more to set our feet on shore, though a very distant one from our own."

My father had service with the steerage passengers on the Sunday several times during the voyage, and also with the cabin passengers two or three times.

They found the colony in a very unsettled and excited state from the gold mania, and provisions and labour of every kind were very dear. For having their hair cut, an operation which they stood much in need of, they had to pay a shilling each.

My father, feeling his mind drawn to visit the first mate on the vessel they came out in, who had fallen into disgrace with the captain through giving way to habits of intemperance since arriving in port, and was now in prison, they went to see him, and were kindly received by the individual. They gave him such advice as seemed called for, and prayed for him at the throne of grace.

" 11th mo. 19th.— * * * In the evening took tea and sat with Henry and Ann Propstring and family."

They attended the Meeting of Friends held in Hobart Town on first day. About thirty were present. In the evening they met a number of convicts, the workmen of their host, who was a tailor, to whom they read a portion of Scripture, and afterwards preached the gospel. They met with a great number of persons who had been sent out to the colony as prisoners of the Crown, whom it was truly sad to see in such a situation. Many of them had been well brought up, and were respectably connected; but generally through the influence of intoxicating drink had fallen, and descended to the position in which my father found them. He was glad to see some, whose terms of imprisonment had expired, doing well, and filling useful stations in society.

" 22nd 11 mo.—This morning proceeded with our family visits. Our first sitting was with ——, a young man at present in the employ of our friend George W. Walker as a porter. He is from Birmingham, in England, had his education at Ackworth School, which institution he left in 1834, and eight years ago was sent out a convict to this colony. My sympathies were deeply awakened on his account, and I felt much for him. Our next was with ——, wife, and daughter, residing on the meeting-house premises. —— was an apprentice with our friend D. H. Smith, of Bradford, married out of the Society, and was eventually sent here as a convict. His family came some years afterwards, since which he has had his sentence commuted. He was tenderly pleaded with in the constrainings of gospel love to submit to the operations of that Spirit which could change his heart and guide his feet into the way of peace, and I trust there was in him an ear to hear, but oh ! that there were in him also a heart to obey. * * *

"It is strange to us in walking along the road to observe the shrubs in the gardens in full bloom in the 11th month. The scarlet geraniums are strikingly beautiful, as well as many kinds of plants which in England are only to be found in greenhouses. Here they flourish in the open air.

"23rd 12th mo.—We have now seen all, as far as we know, who are making profession with us in Van Dieman's Land, and find the whole number of members and attenders of our meetings to be 76, besides some few who occasionally come and sit down with Friends. A large proportion of those in membership are children, as well as several who are attenders only. * * * Since being in the neighbourhood of Launceston, I have heard some painful particulars respecting an individual who was once a member of Brighouse Monthly Meeting, and very respectably connected; but, through yielding to temptation, so far fell away as to be sent out here as a convict, where in the time of his distress friends were raised up for his help, and through their means he was placed in a situation to redeem his character. For a time he did well, but again giving way to temptation, he rapidly sunk from the position he had attained, and departed wider and wider from the right way. He was last heard of at Port Philip, in a very low and degraded condition. The reflections on this mournful case have induced humbling feelings on the frailty and weakness of man in his best estate, and the great need there is for ' him that thinketh he standeth, to take heed lest he fall.'

7th day, 25th.—Left Launceston by the coach this morning at five o'clock for Captain Dixon's, of Skelton Castle, as he has named his residence, which is nothing more than a plain brick building with a castellated parapet. We arrived at Taylor's Gate about eight o'clock,

where we found a conveyance waiting to take us on to
Skelton Castle, which is ten miles from the high road.
Captain Dixon, who is a brother of our friend Esther
Mather, of Hobart Town, both of whom were from Yorkshire, sent us a very kind invitation to pay him a visit;
and although he is not in profession with Friends, yet I
felt a liberty to accept his offer; but no time having been
fixed upon, we found on arrival that he was in Hobart
Town, and not expected back for some days. We were,
nevertheless, kindly received and made cordially welcome
by Robert Crawford, a young man whom Captain D. may
be said to have adopted, having no family of his own.
Here we also found our friend Francis Cotton, whom we
knew was intending to visit Skelton Castle when we
parted from him at Campbelltown on fourth day. We
shall therefore endeavour to reconcile Captain D.'s absence, and probably stay here two or three days, as far as
we see at present. Captain D. has a large establisment,
and one of the finest gardens we have seen in Van
Dieman's Land.

"First day, 26th.—* * * At three in the afternoon
service according to the liturgy of the Church of England
was performed by a clergyman who attends at Captain
D.'s for that purpose every first day. His large parlour
is seated for the occasion, and the families of two or three
settlers in the neighbourhood, and some of the prisoner
servants, usually attend. The clergyman staying to take
tea, we had an opportunity of becoming a little more acquainted with him, and I was agreeably surprised to find
that he was a native of Halifax in Yorkshire, which place
he left about fifteen years ago.

"Second day, 27th.—Walking out this afternoon,
Frederic and myself fell in with a flock of upwards of
two thousand sheep, which three or four men were driving
to a fresh run in the bush. One of the men told us his
master had shorn this season towards twenty thousand.

Some proprietors in Van Dieman's Land, we were told, have a still larger number. The country seems indeed peculiarly adapted for sheep, a small portion of it only being fit for cultivation.

"1st mo. 1st, 1853.—Went to the Penitentiary, or Prisoners' Barracks, to enquire about an individual who was a schoolfellow at Ackworth, but whom I had been informed, to my great sorrow, was now a prisoner of the Crown in this colony. The superintendent informed us that J. G., from some misconduct, had been re-sentenced for six months to Impression Bay, but was expected to be returned to Hobart Town in a few weeks. James Boyd, who is the manager of the institution, very kindly showed us over the extensive premises, and explained to us something of the system of discipline adopted in the establishment. The order and cleanliness which prevailed throughout was matter of admiration, and we could scarcely believe that within these walls were confined from eight hundred to a thousand of the worst characters. * * * Corporal punishment, we were told, is never resorted to on any occasion. Solitary confinement is what they look to as likely to produce more beneficial results.

" Seventh day, 7th.— * * * We afterwards went on to the ' Cascade Factory,' the establishment where the female convicts are received from the vessels in which they are sent out. It is also the prison where they undergo any second sentence to which they may become liable whilst in the colony. There are between five and six hundred confined here at the present time. The superintendent very kindly showed us over the different apartments, and explained to us the present system of discipline, which is found to answer so well, that in general they have but little trouble with them. They are all employed in different sorts of labour and have task work assigned them, and all that they do more than is allotted them is passed to their credit, and goes towards shortening their term of servitude; and it is not uncommon in this way for an individual who is sentenced for seven years to have her liberty at the end of four or five. They are not allowed to converse, silence being enjoined throughout both at work and at meal times, as well as after they retire for the night. The order and cleanliness prevailing throughout all the establishment was gratifying, and a proof of good management on the part of the superintendent. A number of the prisoners of the worst character were in separate cells, where they also had employment of one kind or other, sewing, knitting, spinning, &c., and some few of the most incorrigible were undergoing a few days confinement in solitary cells, in entire darkness, and without employment.

" Second day, 10th.—This forenoon walked over to Newtown, three miles, and went through the Orphan School, a noble institution supported by the Home Government, where between five and six hundred children, from the age of three years to fourteen, are clothed, fed, and educated, and endeavours used to prepare them to become useful members of society. They are nearly all the offspring of convicts, or those who have been deserted by their parents. The girls' side of the house and the infant school department appeared to be under very good management; but the boys were not in that order which was desirable, owing probably to some change in the system of giving instruction, which we were informed was about being introduced. We had an opportunity of hearing about thirty of the elder boys read, and were much pleased with their manner and style, altogether devoid of that tone and drawl which we sometimes meet with. Many of this class were boys of interesting countenances * * * and I felt myself constrained to extend unto them the language of our blessed Saviour, when upon earth He said, ' Suffer little children to come unto me, and forbid them not.' But I had not uttered many sentences before it was intimated that the children of the Roman

Catholics were not allowed to hear anything in the shape of religious instruction from any but those of their own persuasion, and a large proportion of those present being of that class it could not be allowed. * * * The master was very courteous, and seemed to regret that such was the case, and sorrow filled my heart at this evidence of the domination of the Romish clergy, and the means they make use of to keep their people in ignorance of the truth, in order that they may hold their authority over them. But Babylon and her merchandise shall surely be overthrown, for the mouth of the Lord hath spoken it. * *

" We have now seen through all the convict establishments in Hobart Town and its neighbourhood; and, as far as we have been able to judge, the discipline and treatment of the prisoners whilst under the immediate care of the Government authorities is well calculated to encourage good conduct. But when they leave these institutions, and are hired out to the settlers, the great temptations that are set before them through both town and country in the great number of public-houses for the sale of intoxicating drinks, cause many of those who, as long as they could not get these things, were steady, orderly characters, again to break out and commit some crime, which subjects them to the lash of the law. This has appeared to us to be a fearful evil, as well as great injustice on the part of Government to place temptation immediately before the eyes of partially reformed characters, as it is well known the vice of intemperance had in most cases been the cause of bringing them out here as criminals. The paltry sum which is raised as revenue from the sale of these things is much more than expended in the cost of punishing those who are brought into difficulty through their use. In Hobart Town, a place of not more than twenty thousand inhabitants, there are not less than one hundred and eighty licensed houses for the sale of intoxicating drinks, and the number of drunken people we meet in the streets exceeds any thing I ever saw in any other place, which we cannot wonder at when we consider that there is one public-house to every one hundred and ten individuals in the town, and these of a class most likely to fall into temptation."

My father and his companion now sailed for New Zealand, and had a very trying and uncomfortable passage owing to the smallness of the vessel and poor accommodation. They were obliged to give up their cabin, as the smell was so disagreeable from the cattle which were on board as cargo, and the captain kindly gave his own cabin up for their use. Vessels only sailed at long intervals from Hobart Town to New Zealand, so there was no choice as to the ship they went in. They were becalmed for some days, and driven out of their course when within sight of their destination; but at last a pilot came on board, and they anchored safely in the harbour of Wellington, the entrance to which is not very safe, there being a dangerous reef of rocks nearly half way across it.

"31st 1st mo.—Called this morning upon Daniel Wakefield, to whom we had a letter of introduction from our friend Cornelius Hanbury. He and his wife both received us kindly, and on taking our leave D. W. offered his services in any way in which he could be useful to us. On getting back to our quarters, our landlord informed us that Thomas Mason from the Hutt was in town, and would shortly call upon us; and on my going out into the street to purchase an article I was in want of at one of the stores, I very unexpectedly met with him. He appears to be an interesting man, and it was pleasant in this distant land to greet a *friend*. He gave us a kind invitation to his house, and we agreed to go up to the Hutt to-morrow, if nothing unforeseen prevents. * * * Our landlord, Baron Von Alzdorf, is a German, and an

THOMAS MASONS OF THE HUTT, IN WELLINGTON N.Z.

agreeable, interesting man. He was one of the first settlers in the colony, and has seen a thriving town spring up where there was nothing but a forest.

"2nd mo. 1st.—This morning we landed two boxes of books and tracts which we brought with us from Hobart Town, after which we took a walk on the high grounds above the town, from which we had a full view of the harbour and the surrounding neighbourhood. * * * We left Wellington at four o'clock by the van for the district of the Hutt, where our friend Thomas Mason resides. Our conveyance was a rude one, a covered cart on springs, drawn by two horses, one before the other, calculated both for goods and passengers. Our road lay along the shore at the foot of the mountains, where the hill had been cut away just sufficient for the purpose, but in some parts so narrow as not to allow two vehicles to pass each other. On our way we passed several of the huts of the natives, and saw many of them returning to their homes for the night, some of them carrying baskets of potatoes, which they had been getting from their cultivated patches, which we were told form the principal part of their food. * *

"2nd mo. 2nd.—Took a walk this morning for a mile or two up the road, and passed many of the huts of the natives, which are very rude constructions of split timber covered with bark, and so low as to require them to stoop on entering. They are generally surrounded with little patches of cultivated ground, planted with potatoes and maize, and other vegetables, and many of them have good crops of wheat. * * * What is remarkable, and has been told us by all whom we have spoken to on the subject, is the fact that there are no venomous reptiles on the whole island, neither any beasts of prey. * * The only animal in the woods that we have heard of is the wild pig, which has sprung from the two or three left on the island by Captain Cook. They are now very numerous, and are hunted by the natives, and the pork is purchased by the

whites, and forms an article of export. * * * This afternoon Frederic and myself took another walk out into the
bush, and saw several native huts of a ruder kind than we
had before met with, made entirely of bark and a kind of
long grass. In one of them was a man laid on the
ground, smoking his pipe; but the others were empty,
the inmates being out at their work. We took the liberty
to look into some of them, and found them entirely void
of anything like furniture of any kind. Their beds were
nothing more than long grass spread on the ground, on
which they lie down rolled in their blankets. An iron pot
to boil their potatoes in, a frying pan, a calabash or kind
of gourd to drink out of, and a bag or two made of the
New Zealand flax, comprised all their conveniences for
cooking. The fire is made in the middle of the hut, the
smoke making its way out as it can, there being no opening for that purpose except the door by which they enter.

"Some of the trees of the New Zealand forest grow to
a large size. One of these is the Rata, of the parasitical
tribe. It first adheres to some other tree, fastens its
arms around it, and, as it increases in size and strength,
overtops the original tree, which is killed by its rude em-
brace, and takes its room. The tree ferns are also very
fine. We saw one this afternoon at least thirty feet in
height, the stem as thick as a man's body, and its leaves
proportionably large. The 'supple jack,' as it is called,
spreads itself from bush to bush, and although not thicker
generally than a man's finger, is so tough and strong as
to hinder any quick progress through a New Zealand
forest.

"2nd mo. 7th.—This morning after breakfast, having
been furnished with some ham sandwiches by our kind
hostess, Frederic and myself set out for a day's journey
amongst the settlers. We had provided ourselves with
books and tracts, and were kindly received by all upon
whom we called, both natives and whites. We travelled
ten or twelve miles, made upwards of twenty calls, and

reached our quarters again about seven in the evening.
In calling upon the Maories, as the natives are called, we
found great disadvantage from our ignorance of their
language. Still they seemed pleased to see us, and we
left with some of them Maori Testaments, which our
friend Thomas Mason had supplied us with, and which
some of them could read. Many of the older men amongst
them are very much tattooed, their faces being covered
with lines and curves made with the greatest regularity.
A very painful operation, we understood, and which is
now very much out of use with the rising generation.

"Third day, 8th.—Pursued our work in calling upon
the settlers in the Hutt, more immediately in the neighbourhood of our friend Thomas Mason's. We were at
twenty-one houses in the course of the day, and our visits
were kindly received. * * * The day was again very
warm, and I was a good deal fatigued with the exertion
of climbing over logs and fences. * * * Some of the
land we passed over to-day seemed to be very rich and
fertile, clothed with fine pasturage, and yielding abundant crops. We were through a section of a hundred
acres belonging to a relative, which I believe is considered to be equal to most in the valley. It is tenanted
by four families, each occupying twenty-five acres. One
of the tenants had just got up his first planting of
potatoes on little more than a rood of ground, which
had yielded the extraordinary quantity of three tons
and a half, as he himself told us. He had put in a
second crop on the same ground, which he supposed, if
the season was favourable, might produce him an equal
quantity. It is not at all uncommon in this climate
to get two crops in the year.

"Fourth day, 16th.—Proceeded with our work of making calls upon the settlers as before. In the course of
the day we made twenty-three visits. But our work was
cut short by a very unexpected circumstance which took

place just when we were thinking of looking out for some
place where we might get a little dinner, and rest awhile.
Crossing the bridge over the river Hutt, we were met by
a middle-aged man, meanly attired, with a wound on his
face and one of his eyes almost swollen up, suggesting
by his appearance the last night's drunken fray. Supposing him to be a resident here, we made some casual
observation, and were about to pass on, when we observed
him eyeing us closely, and looking earnestly at our basket
of tracts, on which I handed him a couple, when he said
something about our being Friends, and said he was once
a member of our Society. I looked at him incredulously,
and expressed my doubts as to the truth of his statement.
He then said he was from Bradford, and that his name
was ——. Still I could not credit his assertion, until I
mentioned some circumstances which I felt satisfied no
other person could know. We found that he was engaged
in taking care of some horses for a person who had come
to the place the evening before, and had put up at a
public-house we were just about to pass. We went there,
and ordered a little dinner for ourselves, so that we might
have the opportunity of seeing more of him, and making
a little enquiry about him.

"We found that he had been in New Zealand eighteen
months, mostly in the town of Wellington, and that his
engagement with his present employer was just at an
end, and he was thinking of engaging as hostler at the
public-house where we then were, the landlord having
offered to engage him at twelve shillings a week besides
board and lodging. Seeing that it would be a very unsuitable place for one given at times to habits of intemperance, we desired him to relinquish the offer, and try
to get employment in a less-exposed situation. We told
him that we had understood our friend Thomas Mason
was in want of some assistance on his farm, mentioned
its being to-morrow morning the time of their mid-week
Meeting, and received from him a promise that he would
come. Having spent two or three hours with him, we

left him, hoping to see him again to-morrow if the Lord permit; and oh! that we may be the means in the Lord's hand of turning him from the evil of his ways and opening a way of return for him to the Father's house, where there is bread enough and to spare. Mysterious indeed are the ways of Providence, that we should in this very unexpected way meet with this poor wanderer, not having the least idea that he was in this island, and having been unable to hear any recent tidings of him, though frequent inquiry was made while we were in Van Dieman's Land.

" Fifth day, 17th.—Sat down as usual with our friend Thomas Mason's family in their mid-week Meeting. * * I am sorry to say we were disappointed in not seeing the party whom we met with yesterday, nor hearing anything of him, although we were on the look-out for him all the day, and our kind friends here were fully prepared, from our representation of the case, to give him an open reception. * * *

" Sixth day, 18th.—Being unexpectedly prevented going to Wellington by the van this morning as we had intended, our friend Thomas Mason kindly lent Frederic his mare to ride down. We met with ——, but under very discouraging circumstances, giving evidence of his having yielded again to temptation. * * * I intend to use my utmost endeavours to get him to return with me to our friend Thomas Mason's in the evening."

My father had the satisfaction of at length inducing —— to hire himself to Thomas Mason as an assistant on his farm, and there seemed a likelihood of his becoming useful and settled there.

After visiting most of the dwellings of the settlers in the Hutt valley, about two hundred in number, and scattered over a district of ten miles, and leaving books and tracts with them, which were generally very well received, my father and his companion crossed over Cook's Straits in a small craft which happened to be going to "the Wairau," and were met there by a Friend, and taken to his house. They only met with two individuals who had belonged to the Society of Friends. There were but few settlers in this valley, which extended for twenty miles. The houses were mostly of mud, thatched with a kind of long grass. My father left tracts and books with the inmates, who had generally emigrated from England, and seemed to be prospering, after having had to undergo great hardships on first coming out. After staying here three weeks, having been detained waiting for a suitable means of conveyance to Nelson, they at last set out on horseback in company with some others.

"3rd mo. 17th, 1853.—We were five in company, each separately mounted, and equipped with bag and baggage for our wilderness journey. We went briskly along over the Wairau plains for fourteen or fifteen miles, when about one o'clock we halted by the side of a stream, turned our horses loose to graze, minding to secure such of them by tether rope as were disposed to stray, kindled a fire, and boiled some water for tea, which, although without milk, and drunk out of tin pannikins, we found, with the addition of bread and cheese, to be very refreshing. After resting about an hour, we again set out, but had not proceeded far before we found that the Timor pony, a brisk little animal which W. R.'s daughter rode, would be unequal to the journey; and the only way by which the difficulty could be obviated was to call at the first station we should come to, and try to procure another animal in its place, which we did, and were favoured to travel on very well the rest of the day, reaching an empty hut about two miles from Dapper's Station soon after

sunset, where we took up our quarters for the night.
Here we again repeated our repast of bread and cheese;
then, each selecting his resting place, taking off his coat,
and rolling himself up in his blanket, laid down on the
floor, and courted 'nature's sweet restorer, balmy sleep.'
But most of us did this in vain for some time, from the
host of fleas that began to assail us, and the noise of the
rats upon whose privacy we had intruded. The latter
were soon silenced by the presence of a good dog that
was admitted from the outside; but not so the former.

"18th.—About an hour before break of day we were
all stirring, kindled our fire and prepared our breakfast, a
repetition of our last night's meal, and collecting our
horses, which had been grazing through the night around
our hut, by half-past six o'clock were again on our way.
Calling at Dapper's Station, we procured a leg of mutton
for to-day's dinner. Our track lay up the plain for about
ten or twelve miles, until we crossed the Wairau river
and its branches, three or four of which we forded in a
short distance. The water in all of them was low, the
deepest of them not being more than three feet; but the
great rapidity of the stream, and the large boulders com-
posing its bed, render it a very dangerous stream to cross
when at all swollen. And this is very much the character
of the rivers and streams throughout New Zealand: rapid
mountain torrents, many times altogether impassable.
Ten miles from the river we halted for dinner, kindled
our fire under the shade of a bush, and each, at the end
of a forked stick, cooked his chop, and eat it with a slice
of bread, with tea or water fresh from the stream for our
drink. On starting again, the fresh horse which W. R.
procured on the road yesterday showed signs of failing;
and, as we were just entering on the Big Bush, a dense
forest of black birch, nine miles through, it was judged
most prudent to leave him behind, turning him loose on
the plain to shift for himself. And well was it for us
that we did, for our strongest horses were almost finished

by the exertion of getting through this dreaded place, of which it would be altogether useless to try to convey an idea to those who have not seen it.   The trees are cut down for the breadth of five or six yards to afford a passage, and the stumps left standing two or three feet high.   The horses, for great part of the way, plunging their feet at every step into deep mud, from which it is great exertion to draw them out.   This, together with the high banks and deep ravines which are to ascend and descend, make it fearful and fatiguing work both to the horse and his rider.   My companion and W. R., on account of our having to leave one horse behind, had to ride and walk by turns, but the one who walked could generally outstrip him who rode.   The time it took for us to go through was nearly four hours, and glad we were when we emerged out of the gloom of the forest into open day.   Two miles further brought us to David Ker's, a house of accommodation, and the only inhabited dwelling in a distance of fifty miles along this track.   It is a decent mud house, with three or four rooms; but we found it well occupied, no less than fifteen having arrived there before us, going in the opposite direction to ourselves, most of them parties on their return from Nelson races, which were just concluded.   Beds were altogether out of the question.   The floor of one of the rooms and a couple of bunks, as they are called, afforded accommodation to eleven men; the rest were distributed in other parts of the house.   Our place was on the floor; and, although it was hard, it would have been tolerable to me but for the fleas, which annoyed me so unmercifully for some time that I gave up all hopes of sleep, but towards morning I got a little rest.

" We were all stirring by daylight.   On going outside and looking about for some means of washing, I was referred by our host to the river at a short distance, and on going down to it found some of my fellow-travellers there before me performing their morning ablutions.

Having secured a little breakfast and caught our horses, by eight o'clock on the morning of the 19th we were on the road up the mountains, a high range of which we had to cross, as well as several smaller ones in the course of the day. New Zealand is peculiarly a land of mountains and valleys, of rivers and streams, our full share of which we passed in this day's journey, which was long and fatiguing. Twenty-two miles from David Ker's we came to another house kept for the accommodation of travellers, which was a welcome sight to us, being both weary and hungry; and I believe I might venture to say, that we did full justice to the good fare that our hostess placed before us. * * * From this place, which is called Fox Hill, we had a ride of seventeen miles through a district of country which may be called settled, the land being partly fenced in, and neat little dwellings erected at short distances, which was a truly pleasant sight to the eye, after the wilderness we had passed through. It was eight o'clock when we reached Richmond, a village eight miles from Nelson. Our horses, as well as ourselves, were completely done up, having travelled in the three days no less than a hundred and ten miles, and great part of the way the road difficult as well as dangerous. May thankfulness fill my heart unto our great Preserver, who hath brought us safely through this perilous journey, seeking day by day for ability to do His holy will!"

After resting a day or two to recruit themselves after their arduous journey, they went on to Nelson, and took up their quarters at an hotel, none of the Friends being in a position to accommodate them.

"In the evening we took tea with Martha Strong, whose husband, Samuel Strong, is at present from home on business at Melbourne. They have two children—a daughter nearly grown up, and a little boy about four

years of age. Our friend Martha Strong has been suffering some time under what seems likely to be an incurable
disease; yet, in spending a few hours with her, the
cheerful resignation of her spirit to the chastening hand
of a merciful Creator was comforting to my mind. Before
we left to return to our lodgings, we were favoured to fall
into silence, and a precious covering was felt to prevail
over us, under which the language of encouragement was
handed forth to our dear friend still to cast her burden
upon the Lord, in the humble belief that He was near to
sustain her.

"28th.—Called this morning upon the ministers of
the Episcopal, Catholic, and Scotch Churches, by all of
whom we were well received. We also made a call at
the dwelling of the Baptist minister, but did not find him
at home. Our Friends here having expressed to us their
wish to have a meeting house, believing that if such was
the case some parties might come to sit down with them
who do not feel freedom to do so when the meeting is
held in a private dwelling, my companion and myself
waited upon C. A. Dillon, the Government land agent
here, to enquire if there was a suitable plot still in the
hands of the Crown which could be granted to Friends
for the purpose of building a meeting house upon, all other
denominations having had grants for that use. He received us very courteously, and seemed quite disposed to
forward the views of Friends as far as he was concerned;
but said that on account of the fewness of our numbers in
Nelson at present, the Governor, with whom the decision
would rest, might possibly feel a little difficulty in making
the grant. At the same time he pointed out one or two
allotments as the likeliest remaining in the hands of
Government, and did not appear to think there was any
objection to our applying for one of them if Friends here
thought them suitable for the purpose. In the afternoon
our friends Martha Strong and Isaac Hill accompanied us
to look at the lots. They were neither of them exactly

A NOONDAY HALT IN MOTUEKA VALLEY — N.Z.

such as we should have chosen had there been more for choice; and it is left for our Friends here to consider which will suit them best, the agent kindly allowing us a few days to decide upon it. * * *

"3rd mo. 29th.—Having felt a drawing towards the settlement of Motueka, across the bay, about forty miles from Nelson, we concluded to set out on foot, in order to afford us an opportunity of calling upon the settlers on the road. We accordingly left Nelson to-day about noon. * * The weather was warm, and we found it a great relief to put our luggage on an empty bullock dray which overtook us on the road, and to ride part of the way on the same conveyance, giving the driver a few tracts and a small book as an acknowledgment for his kind accommodation. * * *

"30th.—This morning the weather was beautifully fine. We had our breakfast early, and started off on our journey each loaded with his own baggage, Frederic also carrying a small basket of tracts and books for distribution by the way. After travelling a few miles we came upon the Wairau River, a considerable stream, which we were consulting how we should pass, when a bullock dray came up and helped us over. After passing this river we trudged along with our loads which were beginning to feel pretty heavy from the increasing heat, when, to our great relief, we were overtaken by an empty bullock dray, and two men riding upon it. We asked the liberty to ride, which was readily granted. The men soon began to enquire if we had anything in our bags to sell. We told them we had not; but we had some tracts and books to give. They replied they would 'not have them,' and said they were 'not wanted in this country,' and they were 'nothing worth;' and railed a good deal against both us and our books. We replied to their charges as well as we were able, but all to no purpose. They became more and more irritated against us, and at

last the elder of the men said he considered it a sin to
let us ride on his bullock dray, and told the younger to
stop and let us get off, which we told him we would do
at once if he desired it. The younger man, who was
driving, seemed more moderate, and was not willing to
stop, but drove on until our roads parted, when he told
us which way to go, and how we were to do to get across
the Waieta River, which was at a short distance. We
gave the young man some tracts, which he received; but
the old man was still very violent, and insisted on our
paying him two shillings for riding on his dray the distance of about a mile. I then felt it my duty to speak
very seriously to him respecting his conduct, as did also
my companion, which appeared to have some effect upon
him. To our satisfaction he began to soften a little, and
he received a tract from us, shook hands with us, and we
bade him farewell. We had not gone many yards from
the place before he called out to us to come back, and get
into his dray again, and he would go with us through the
river, an offer which we thankfully accepted, and found
that it would have been difficult to get over if he had not
done so. Thus the Lord worked for us to our great admiration; and well is it to trust in Him at all times, for
He can turn the hearts of the children of men as it
pleaseth Him." * * *

My father called upon the settlers in the Waimea and
Motueka districts, often walking long distances in the
day, over mountain ranges, and sometimes finding no
water to quench their thirst. They appointed some
meetings, and found a few persons who had been connected with, or members of the Society of Friends; but
who now made no profession of belonging to them, and
who nevertheless received my father very kindly, and
did all in their power to assist him in any way they
could.

" Motueka, 4th mo. 9th.—On walking out last evening about sunset, we heard a strange howling noise in the direction of the ' pah,' or native village, about half a mile from our quarters, and on enquiry were informed that they were lamenting for one of their dead, and that they sometimes carried it to such a length as to be quite an annoyance to the neighbourhood. A few days ago, in passing their ' pah,' we had an opportunity of seeing their manner of cooking. In a hole dug in the ground to the depth of about two feet, and four or five feet in diameter, they had kindled a fire of wood, in which they had heated a quantity of stones. Upon these stones they laid a number of pumpkins, and then over these some more heated stones, then from one to two bushels of potatoes, and on the top of these a quantity of dried eels. All this was then carefully covered around with grass and green stalks, and some water sprinkled over it, which caused a strong steam to arise. The whole was then covered up with mats, and out of a hole which the women who were preparing the food dug with two long pointed sticks, a quantity of earth was spread over it to the thickness of several inches, effectually preventing the escape of any steam or heat. When they judge the mess to be sufficiently cooked, the earth, &c., is removed, and they sit down round about it, and all help themselves."

My father and his companion returned to Nelson in a small craft which plied between Motueka and Nelson, across the bay.

" 11th.—The funeral of an individual had taken place in Nelson this afternoon whose death had caused a great sensation. His name was Thomas Smith, one of the principal inhabitants of the place, in good circumstances, middle-aged, and about to retire from business, that of a brewer, which he had carried on in an extensive way. It was just the end of the hop gathering, when the

women employed in picking the hops have the custom of
throwing any man who may come into the hop grounds
into the hop bin, and covering him over with hops, which
they had taken the liberty of doing with their master,
and of also pushing a woman down upon him whilst he
was in the bin, by which he sustained an internal injury
which caused his end in less than two days, verifying in
a striking and remarkable manner the language of Holy
Writ, ' In the midst of life we are in death.'

" Fourth day, 13th.—Employed the fore part of the
day in calling upon some of the settlers in the outskirts
of the town.   In the afternoon went to look at a plot of
ground which had belonged to J. S. Cotterell, the young
man belonging to our Society who lost his life in the
Wairau massacre, and which it was thought might be
more suitable as a site for a meeting-house than either
of the lots which had been pointed out by the Government agent, as yet in the hands of the Crown.   There is
an acre of ground and a small cottage upon it, which,
although not in very good repair, it was thought might,
at a trifling expense, be made available as a meeting-
house for the present.   The whole might be had, we
understand, for £50.   There are some objections to it on
account of its being on the side of a hill, but still there
is a sufficient space of flat to answer the purpose for
the present, not only for a meeting-house but also for a
burying ground.   On the whole it seemed to us the most
eligible site that had offered; but there being some little
diversity of opinion about it, nothing has yet been decided
upon.

" Seventh day, 16th.—Believing that it may tend to
the advantage of the few members of our Society who
reside here, we have agreed to purchase the property
under consideration for the sum of £50, myself becoming
answerable for the payment thereof, with the intention of
transferring it over to trustees for the use of the Society,

FRIENDS MEETING HOUSE   NELSON   N.Z.

if approved of by the Meeting for Sufferings in London. The expense of fencing the ground, and repairing the cottage so as to make it suitable to meet in, together with the expenses attendant on the purchase, will in all probability amount to £20 more. It has been a matter of serious consideration to take upon myself the responsibility of such a step; but the circumstances of the case appearing to call for it, and having the full unity of my dear companion, I did not feel as if I should be justified in shrinking from it, trusting that it may meet with the approbation of our Friends in England, and that some of them to whom the Lord hath intrusted much of this world's goods will cheerfully come forward and assist in bearing the burden.

"Third day, 19th.—My companion and myself have both been busily engaged, along with our two workmen, in laying out the path up to the cottage proposed to be used as a meeting-house, and levelling the ground in front of it, &c. Our friend Martha Strong came to look at us this afternoon, and seemed much pleased at the progress we had made. It was to me an affecting circumstance to see her on the premises, she herself having expressed her expectation of being the first to be interred there, which from present circumstances may seem not to be improbable.

"Third day, 26th.—Have believed it in the way of my duty to take private opportunities to speak to one or two individuals who are staying at the Wakatu on the recklessness of their conduct, as well as to the landlord and landlady in allowing the guests to go on in the disorderly manner in which they do. It was a trying service, and I am not sanguine of its producing any good effects; but I feel satisfied in the endeavour to discharge what appeared to be my duty in this respect. We also called upon Major Richmond, and laid before him the observations that had been forced upon our view as regards the large

G

number of individuals, particularly young men, who are in the habit of spending their time at the public-houses in rioting and drinking in this settlement. He received our remarks with attention, and expressed his regret that it was so, and his willingness and his desire to discourage it as far as lay in his power.

"5th mo. 13th.—Completed the work at the cottage, and have got two or three short forms or seats into it. It is a nice little place, quiet and retired, still very near the town, being almost all that we could wish for the purpose intended. In the belief that we have now nearly got through the little service required of us in this neighbourhood, we have made some enquiry about horses to take us back to the Wairau; but I regret to say hitherto without success.

"1st day, 5th mo. 15th, 1853.—This morning we held our meeting for the first time in the meeting-house; present, nine individuals, six adults and three children. It was a very interesting occasion as being the first time Friends had met in a place appropriated to the purpose, and I am thankful in the belief that the Lord condescended to own our little company by the tokens of His presence. * * *

"Fourth day, 18th.—Have made arrangements with our landlord to lend us two horses to go to the Wairau, for which we are to pay him the sum of £7, and look towards leaving Nelson on sixth day, if the Lord permit. The prospect of leaving our dear friend Martha Strong under the peculiar circumstances in which she is placed feels very trying; yet apprehending we have got through our little service here, I do not feel as if we should be warranted in prolonging our stay, now that we have met with horses for our journey.

"5th mo. 20th.— * * * Went to breakfast at our

friend Martha Strong's, after which we had a precious
parting opportunity with her and her family. It was
very close work to me to leave this our dear friend, unto
whom my heart had become united in tender and affectionate sympathy; but comforting was the belief, that
there were bonds which neither time nor distance, nor
death itself can sever, and earnestly do I desire that I
may be so kept by the power of Divine grace, that when
my time of probation on earth is ended, I may become
united in the realms of bliss to those who, like this our
precious sister, have come out of great tribulation, and
had their robes washed and made white in the blood of
the Lamb, and will therefore be permitted to stand before
the throne of God, and to serve him night and day in
His temple. After a sojourn of about two months in this
neighbourhood, and having discharged the little service
required of us, about noon we took what I believe to be
our final departure from Nelson." * * *

After passing the Big Bush on their return journey to
Wellington, through which they had a guide, my father
and his companion proceeded on horseback.

" On emerging from the Big Bush we opened on to an
extensive grassy plain, where we halted nearly an hour
to let our horses feed, and to refresh ourselves with a
little bread and cheese and fresh water from the brook.
We then went on at a pretty good pace for about ten
miles, when we came to the Wairau River, which we
forded in three branches, at the same place where a few
weeks previously C. A. Dillon, the Government Land
Commissioner, had lost his life. The stream where we
crossed was not more than three feet deep; neither was
it higher, that we could understand, when this valued
individual was carried away; but the rippling of the
waters over a bed of large boulder stones, on which it
was difficult for our horses to maintain their footing, and

the rapidity of the stream, were such as to render both Frederic and myself quite unconscious for a time of the direction in which our horses were moving, or whether they were moving at all. This may seem incredible to those unacquainted with the New Zealand rivers, or more properly torrents, as they may truly be called; but I may acknowledge it was cause of thankfulness when we had safely crossed this river and another called the Branch, about four miles beyond it, considered equally dangerous. About two hours after crossing the latter we came to Duppa's Station, the first habitation of man we had seen since leaving our last night's resting place. Here all travellers stop on their way from Nelson to the Wairau, and are allowed to spread their blankets for the night, and to turn their horses out to feed. They are also provided gratis, as they are at all the stations, with the usual fare of tea, mutton, and bread. George Duppa is a man of fortune, who came out on the first establishment of the colony, and has now large possessions of flocks and herds; yet the rude way in which he is obliged to live in such an out-of-the-way place, appears to be far from congenial to him, and he talks of returning to England as soon as he can make the needful arrangements for it. There is no female on the establishment.

"Fourth day, 25th.—This morning we dismissed our guide, after paying him £1 for his two days' services, and set out by ourselves. Our road lay down the grassy plains of the Wairau, with high mountain ranges on either side, so that there was no probability of our losing our way very far; yet, as the track in many places was very indistinct, we sometimes got out of our road, and came upon a bog or a swamp which we could not pass, and had to retrace our steps for some distance. * * *

"Fifth day, 26th.—We left Bryder's Station about nine o'clock, expecting to have an easy day's journey to William Budge's at the Boulder Bank; but the sequel

proved otherwise. We got down to our friend William
Robinson's about noon, where we learnt that a small
vessel called the 'Old Jack' was at the mouth of the
Wairau, intending to sail in a day or two for Wellington.
I had all along looked towards crossing the Straits in this
vessel, though altogether ignorant of her being in the
river at this time. On learning this, we therefore felt
the necessity of hastening forward. We were told that
owing to the late heavy rains we could not get through
the way we should have to go on horseback; yet as the
weather had been fine for some days we felt inclined to
try. We got on very well for some miles; but on coming
to a gully, the descent into which was down a very steep
bank which had been partly washed away by the stream,
one of our horses could not be induced by all the means
we used to go over it. After toiling with him for at least
half an hour, we were at last obliged to give it up, and
return to the Beaver Station, from whence a boat was expected to go down the river in the morning with some
produce. On our way back to the station, the horse on
which I rode, in crossing a small stream a few inches
deep, suddenly sunk to the top of his legs in mud, from
which it seemed for a time it would be very difficult for
him to extricate himself. But fortunately, before I had
time to throw myself off his back, he gave a spring, and
got a footing upon firm ground. I considered it a providential escape for myself as well as for the poor animal,
as it was more than probable, if I had got off his back,
which I was about to do, the horse in floundering about
might have rolled upon me and buried me in the mud, in
which I should have been quickly suffocated. There was
no one at the station but a Maori woman, the men having
gone down the river, and not being expected to return
until late at night. We sent our horses back from here
to William Robinson's, where they were to be left, by a
boy who had come with us to show us the way, expecting
to pass the night at the station. The Maori woman,
though unable to understand our language, or at least to

exchange many words with us, was very kind. She set
before us some boiled pork and potatoes and two pots of
tea, and invited us to help ourselves; and in the evening,
on making known our desire to lie down, showed us
where to spread our blankets, doing her best to make us
comfortable. We had not been more than an hour or two
in bed before the boatmen arrived, and brought word that
the 'Old Jack' would sail for Wellington by the next
morning's tide. On considering the matter, there seemed
to be no alternative but to get the boatmen to take us
down the river in the night, which, after some persuasion,
they consented to do, as the moon was just about full,
and the weather clear and fine. We set out about eleven
o'clock. The distance was twelve miles. The men had
to row all the way; but, as the tide was in our favour, we
made it in about three hours. The night, although fine,
was cold; and, although we were wrapped up in our
blankets, we felt the exposure a good deal.

"Sixth day, 27th.—* * * Went on board the 'Old
Jack,' the sails of which were quickly unfurled, and in a
few minutes we were under weigh, and soon lost sight of
the Boulder Bank. The wind not being fair for our running across the straits, our captain made for Port Under-
wood, a harbour in Cloudy Bay, where his family reside,
intending to wait there until the wind should change.
Although it was not pleasant to be detained, yet I felt
thankful under present circumstances to have a little rest
on land. The last few days of hard travelling and loss of
rest had brought on a severe headache and loss of appetite, so that when we landed I could scarcely hold up my
head. Our captain's dwelling did not afford many comforts; yet both he and his wife were disposed to do their
best to make our detention tolerable. Captain Gnard had
known better days; and in the evening he was giving us
an account of his being cast away in the year 1834 on
the eastern coast of the Northern Island of New Zealand, when he and his crew, consisting of nearly thirty

individuals, after escaping the dangers of the sea, were attacked by the natives, who killed and devoured eleven of their number, the rest, except his wife and two children, who were taken captives, with difficulty making their escape to some of the friendly settlements. The captain afterwards found his way to Sydney, where he represented his case to the Governor, who sent a vessel of war and an armed force to demand the restitution of his wife and children. The natives unfortunately refused to give them up until forcible means were used, which cost the lives of a number of New Zealanders; but in the end, the poor woman and her children, after a captivity of five months, were restored to the husband's and parent's arms.

"Second day, 30th.—Soon after midnight a breeze sprung up in our favour; but the night being cloudy, and land not far distant, our captain was afraid to avail himself of it till the day began to break, when the wind increased, and carried us forward at a pretty brisk rate to our desired haven, where we cast anchor soon after nine o'clock; and a great relief it was to be released from the inconvenience and discomforts of the 'Old Jack,' and to get on shore to Baron Alzdorf's, where, after a good wash and a comfortable breakfast, we felt quite revived. Thus, after a perilous journey of ten days from Nelson, wherein we have had to encounter dangers from the wilderness, dangers from the mountain torrents, and dangers from the sea, the Lord hath been mercifully pleased to shield us from harm on every hand. * * Nor can I do less than mark His directing hand in the time of our leaving Nelson so as to arrive at the Wairau just in time for the sailing of the 'Old Jack,' instead of having to wait several weeks for a passage, as we might have had to do in all probability if we had missed this vessel. All these things I am sensible lay me under the greater obligations more faithfully to serve Him who is thus pleased to make bare His almighty arm for the help of a very weak and unworthy one; and oh! saith my soul, that in a future day these favours may not add to my condemnation.

"Wellington, 6th mo. 5th.—About four o'clock this morning we experienced a smart shock of an earthquake. There have been several slight ones felt in this colony within the last three months, and the one we had last night, according to our friend Thomas Mason's account, was the severest they have felt for some years. I was lying awake at the time. The motion was very rapid and shook the house considerably, making it creak a good deal, being a strong frame building well put together; but no damage was done that we know of. The shock did not last more than a few seconds. This is the second that I have been sensible of since I have been in New Zealand, and both in the night, yet of an entirely different character: the one a gentle vibrating motion, and the other rapid and violent.

"6th.—This afternoon Frederic and myself rode over to the Pitoni Pah, in order to see the old chief Opony, whom we met with last week at E. G. Wakefield's. There are about one hundred Maories who reside at this pah in different huts. The house where Opony resides is a frame building of a small size with two rooms in it and a couple of bedsteads, and several conveniences after the European style. Not being able to speak their language, and having no interpreter, we could only converse by signs, which was but little; still they seemed pleased with our visit.

"Sixth day, 10th.— * * * On our reaching the Barracks we went to the 'Orderly Room,' as it is called, to inform the colonel and adjutant that we had seen the chaplain, and received his sanction to distribute some tracts amongst the soldiers. He seemed surprised, and still expressed his doubts as to its being admissible, according to instructions received from home on the sub-

HUTS & GRANARY OF THE NATIVES OF NEW ZEALAND.

ject; but said he would refer to them, and communicate his final opinion to us in a note to be left at our quarters. I think his fear seemed to be lest anything in our tracts should militate against war. We told him that we did not propose to distribute any amongst the soldiers that bore directly upon the subject; but at the same time were ready fully to admit that the free reception of the truth of Christianity would lead to the same thing. On our coming out of the Orderly Room one of the officers followed us, and expressed a desire to have some of our tracts, which we very readily gave him, for which he wished to pay; but on our letting him know that we did not take anything for them, he expressed himself much obliged, and said he should make use of them and distribute them.

" 13th.— * * * The Roman Catholics have a considerable establishment here, and a school for boys and girls, together with a convent for young women. We called upon them, and were introduced to the Bishop, who was very attentive and ready to show us over the premises, every part of which was in very nice order. They had nearly twenty native girls and half-castes, who were taught the English language, some of whom could speak it well. I showed the Bishop, who was a Frenchman, my certificate, which he read over attentively, and on taking leave of him he said he should remember me and pray for me. I offered him a book illustrative of our principles, which he looked over, but said he must be excused accepting. We parted in a friendly manner.

" Third day, 14th.—Visited the jail, or common prison, a very poor place, and altogether unsuitable and inadequate for the purpose. Felons, debtors, and lunatics being altogether,—seventeen inmates on the whole, of whom five were lunatics, there being no establishment in the colony for their reception. A large building is in progress for the new jail, where there will be room for

classification; but the present establishment is a disgrace
to the settlement. We left some tracts with the prisoners and with some soldiers who were keeping guard,
with which they seemed pleased. We afterwards called
upon E. Wheeler, chaplain to the 65th regiment, and left
with him a quantity of tracts for distribution among the
soldiers, not being ourselves allowed to go through the
Barracks for that purpose. We also presented him with
a copy of J. J. Gurney's ' Peculiarities.' We have also
placed in the library of the Wellington Athenæum, 'Mary
Capper's Memoirs,' Penn's 'No Cross No Crown,' Bates'
' Doctrines of Friends,' and the ' Principles of Christianity Vindicated.'

   " 18th.—Fell in to-day with Captain Henry Williams,
who has come out to this colony as agent to a company
in London who are wishing to establish steam navigation
here. He seems at present rather discouraged at his
prospect of success, owing to the apathy of the commer-
cial part of the community on the subject. * * *

   " 20th.—* * * The time seems to be drawing on when
we may be permitted to take our departure from the
shores of New Zealand, and this morning I felt at liberty
to enquire at one of the shipping agent's offices if there
was any vessel likely before long to sail for Sydney, this
having appeared to me to be the next place to aim at.
They informed me there was no vessel at present laid on
for that port, but that one was expected in a few days,
which would probably return to Sydney in a short time.
I do not see much more public service that may be required of me in this colony, unless it be the holding of a
meeting for worship in the large Wesleyan Chapel in
Wellington, which has at times been presented to my
view, but not with that clearness which would warrant
my moving in it, and if I might be excused I should
esteem it a favour, my nature very much shrinking from it;
still I trust to be able to be resigned to the Lord's will.

" Second day, 27th —The roads or streets in Wellington, from the long-continued wet, are in such a state as to render it quite a formidable task to get from one end of the town to the other, unless a person makes up his mind to flounder through both thick and thin. It is almost impossible for loaded vehicles to get along at any rate, and the passenger vans from the Hutt have for some weeks past given up coming into the town; but stop at the outskirts. The footpaths, if such they can be called, being nothing more in most places but one side of the road, are so deep in mud that it requires very close attention to pick our way through it; and this cannot be done even in the daytime without getting up to the shoe tops in many places, and in the evenings there is no alternative but plunging through the best way we can, there being no lamps in the streets except those put out by the hotels and inns, the law requiring that each of these shall show a light over their doors. * *

" Third day, 28th.—Our friend Dr. Prendergast, who has paid considerable attention to the state of the weather in this colony, states that the quantity of rain has been steadily increasing for some years, and that within the last twelve months the depth which has fallen has been 67 inches in the town of Wellington. * * The cattle are accustomed to run out all the winter. The grass is green all the year round, as well as all the native trees and shrubs. English forest trees and fruit trees cast their leaves as with us; but the roses are in bloom through the winter, as well as many other garden plants and shrubs.

" Third day, 5th.—* * After a sojourn of five months in New Zealand, we are not on the whole favourably impressed with the fineness of the climate, at least as regards the Wellington district, further than that it appears, as far as our observation has extended, to be a very healthy one for Europeans, as well as for the children born here. These, with little exception, have a very robust appearance, which was peculiarly striking on our coming from Van Dieman's Land, where the young people generally look delicate and slender. The climate of the Nelson district is pleasant and agreeable, not subject to the high winds they have in Wellington, neither have they so much wet. Of the two, I think it a much more preferable settlement as a place of residence.

"Fifth day, 14th.—This morning we made a call upon the Governor, Sir George Grey, and had a pleasant interview with him. He appears to be an agreeable and interesting man, but heavily burdened with the cares of governing a dissatisfied and uneasy colony, which he is on the point of leaving for England on a professed leave of absence, but probably with the intention of never returning."

After a tedious voyage of more than three weeks, our travellers came in sight of Sydney.

"Fourth day, 10th.—On going up on deck this morning, it was pleasant to find our barque ploughing her way with her head direct to our wished-for port, from which, by noon, our captain reported us not more than fifty miles distant. Our breeze continued through the day, and towards evening, on our nearing the Heads of Port Jackson, it blew very fresh, and at the same time was thick and foggy, with heavy rain, so that it was difficult for our seamen to discern the land. About seven in the evening we got sight of the lighthouse on the South Head, and made signals for a pilot, but without effect; and the night threatening to be very stormy, our captain felt himself constrained to go in without one, both himself and his mate being well acquainted with this coast. As we advanced we continued to show signal lights every two or three minutes, until we approached a reef called the 'Sow and Pigs,' off which a lightship is moored. Just at this juncture we got sight of the pilot boat putting off to us

SMYTH'S, DARLING POINT, — SYDNEY

on the shore, on which our captain ordered the sails
back, in order to take him on board; but in doing so,
the tide, which was very strong, together with the wind,
carried us directly toward the reef, and on the wrong side
the lightship to that on which the channel was. The
danger was imminent; but we were so close to the lightship that we were obliged to keep on our course betwixt
it and the rocks, on which all who were aware of their
situation expected us every moment to strike; but a
watchful Providence carried us safely through, although
it was said that a vessel of our size had never passed
there before, and one a few years ago got on this same
reef, and all on board were lost. Soon after passing the
'Sow and Pigs' the pilot got on board, and took us down
to our anchorage off Penchgut Island, where we lay all
night.

" On the morning of fifth day, 11th, we were up by
daylight to get a view of the harbour, which I suppose is
one of the finest in the world. The sight of the ship-
ing, and the town of Sydney, gave us the impression of
a metropolis which we could not mistake, and which was
still further increased when we went on shore and saw
the business appearance of the streets, and the splendour
of the shops, many of which would equal what we see in
Regent and Oxford Streets, London.

" Third day, 16th.—Lodged last night at Samuel
Smyth's. After breakfast, he went into town as usual to
business, and left us to spend the day with his wife. The
weather was cool and pleasant, the thermometer ranging
not more than about 60°. Frederic and myself feeling
inclined for a walk, we concluded to try to reach the
South Head, distant from our friends' about five miles,
which we accomplished, and got back in time for dinner
at two o'clock. I scarcely remember having a finer walk.
The road, which was very good, lay along the shores of
Port Jackson, affording a beautiful view of its various

coves and of the shipping; and the trees and shrubs
which extended nearly to the water's edge, were beautiful
to look upon, many of them in flower, although only just
past midwinter. From the South Head, upon which is
noble lighthouse and a signal station, there is a beautiful
view of the town of Sydney, at the head of the bay, distant eight miles. There were two or three vessels sailing
up from the Heads, and a seventy-four gun ship called
the 'Hercules' anchored just within, waiting for the tide
to take her up to the town. There are many noble man-
sions scattered all along the road from Sydney to within
two or three miles of the South Head, fully equal to
what we see in the suburbs of our most thriving towns in
England. * * *

"Second day, 22nd.—On settling our last week's account with our landlady, we find that our expenses for
board and lodging amount to 7s. a day each, which is a
good deal, and we would gladly lessen it if we could tell
how. For salt butter we have to pay 3s. per pound, for
ham 1s. 6d., and bacon 1s. 2d., and many other articles
in proportion. For a little blue milk, or more properly
milk and water, to put into our tea, we pay 1s. 6d. per
week. Bread we have very good, and at a moderate price,
7d. the two pound loaf. Vegetables are high, 6d. and 9d.
for a cabbage, and potatoes in proportion.

"9th mo. 1st, 1858.—* * * This afternoon we experienced something of the hot wind, which at times is so
very trying here, accompanied with clouds of fine dust
which penetrate everywhere, the closest windows and
doors proving no barrier to it. In conversation with
different parties since our arrival in Sydney, we find it
to be a fact that the most wealthy citizens are those who
were sent out here as convicts or their descendants, some
of whom have amassed large properties in land and buildings, which from the late increase in value in consequence
of the gold discoveries, have advanced at an enormous

rate. Still we understand this class of persons do not in general find their way amongst the respectable part of the community, who have come out to the colony under different circumstances; though the line of demarcation may not be so distinct as it was.

" 9th mo. 15th.—We have now been five weeks in Sydney, and have had but one day's rain, though we understood before our arrival here they had a very wet time. The weather has certainly been very delightful since we came here, but I suppose the hot weather will shortly set in, which is very trying. Hitherto we have both been favoured with uninterrupted good health, which is a favour we cannot too highly appreciate, particularly the poor traveller far from home and its comforts, and his lot cast among strangers.

" The state of things in this colony is anything but satisfactory, and the recent discoveries of some rich gold mines, which have been reported within the last fortnight, have contributed to rekindle the excitement which before that seemed to be subsiding. It is exceedingly difficult for the captains of vessels to keep their men. They are continually deserting, and refuse to accept as much as £10 or £12 a month wages. Labour of every kind is very high, stonemasons and carpenters wanting from fifteen shillings to twenty shillings a day, which is a great deal, and the hearing of it may perhaps tempt many a workman from England, who is only earning four shillings or five shillings, or less than that. But let them beware of being deceived by the sound of high wages. Rents, and every other thing they need, are high in proportion. As far as I have seen and heard, the steady workman in England, with four shillings or five shillings a day, is every way better off than he would be here with from fifteen shillings to twenty shillings.

" Sixth day, 30th.—Providing ourselves with a lot of tracts and putting some dry biscuits in our pockets, soon

after breakfast we set out on a day's excursion to Botany
Bay. The weather was very warm, and the road in some
parts a deep sand, open and exposed to the burning
sun, which fatigued us a good deal, so that on reaching
the end of our journey, which we did about two o'clock,
we concluded to stay all night at the hotel there which
bears the name of Sir Joseph Banks, one of the companions of Captain Cook in his discovery of Botany Bay.
The gardens and grounds about the inn are laid out with
great taste, and kept in nice order. They have also a
collection of birds and beasts peculiar to this country, as
well as some others, which render the place additionally
attractive to visitors, many of whom come out from
Sydney to spend a little time here.   There is also convenience for bathing, though the water near the shore is in
general shallow, very different to Port Jackson, where
vessels of one thousand tons may anchor within twenty
or thirty yards of the shore.   We much enjoyed a stroll
on the beach, and Frederic had a dip in the sea." * * *

My father and his companion went by steamer to some
settlements on the Hunters' River, where they spent about
three weeks, and met with several Friends, or those who
had been such.   The names of James Backhouse and
George Washington Walker were often mentioned to
them, as being remembered by many whom they visited,
when those Friends visited this country about twenty
years before.   My father mentions partaking of oranges,
fresh picked from the trees, which grew in the garden of
an individual they visited, which he much enjoyed, and
the orange and lemon trees covered with blossom and
ripe fruit at the same time, emitted a most delicious
fragrance.

" Sydney, 11th mo. 10th.—This afternoon went out
again to distribute tracts through a portion of the city

inhabited mostly by the lower classes, amongst whom they were in general thankfully, and in many cases eagerly received. It is a simple service, but one which brings us at times into contact with individuals where we least expect it, in whose minds there is an openness to receive a word of counsel, which may, through the Divine blessing, yield fruits of increase at a future day.

" Sixth day, 11th.—This forenoon waited upon E. Deas Thomson, the Colonial Secretary, to enquire respecting the application for a grant of a piece of ground for the purpose of building a meeting-house upon, which was presented to the Government several weeks since, but to which no answer had yet been given. He informed us that the subject had been brought under consideration two or three times, and that it had now assumed a more favourable aspect than it had at first, and that it was his intention at once to lay it before the Governor, and to let Friends have an answer without delay. The afternoon was again employed in the distribution of tracts, in which it is our endeavour to visit the lowest and worst parts of the city, and truly in this place abounding with wealth, as it does at present, there is a great deal of squalid wretchedness and destitution, arising no doubt in most cases from habits of recklessness and intemperance. Probably no place in the world presents more disgusting and loathsome objects than are to be met with here under the form of women, shocking as they do every remembrance of what is lovely and attractive in the female character.

" First day, 13th.— * * * Our attention has been increasingly turned within the past week to the consideration of the propriety of endeavouring to establish a meeting for discipline among Friends here. Our friend G. W. Walker, in a letter recently received from him, brought the subject weightily before us, and appears to think it a necessary step in order to the safe standing of

the few who seem to be disposed to gather together. On
mentioning the subject to some of those whom we may
consider as likely to be burden-bearers amongst them, we
found their minds more prepared to take hold of the
subject than we had looked for, and on consulting a little
together, it has been concluded to invite such as are
members of the Society to meet together on fourth day
evening to take the matter under their serious consideration. May the Lord be pleased to be a spirit of judgment to those that sit in judgment, that His will and
counsel may be known and followed, and not man's.

"Fourth day, 16th.—At seven o'clock this evening
ten members of the Society assembled, and after solid
and deliberate consideration came to the conclusion to
establish a meeting for discipline in Sydney, to be held
once a month; the first to be on fourth day evening, the
14th of 12th month, at seven o'clock; and no more suitable place offering, it was concluded for them to meet at
our friend Samuel Darton's."

My father being desirous of attending the Yearly Meeting at Hobart Town, Van Dieman's Land, left Sydney
on the 25th of 11th mo., and arrived at Hobart Town
in time to be at its sittings; the meeting having been
postponed for a few days in expectation of R. L.'s and
F. M.'s coming. It was attended by about sixteen
adults. After staying two weeks in Hobart Town,
and being kindly entertained at the house of George
Washington Walker, and visiting the Friends, attending
meetings, &c., R. L. and F. M. proceeded to Tasman's
Peninsula, wishing to visit a former member of the
Society of Friends who was stationed at one of the
penal settlements there. Having reached Impression
Bay by steamer,

"We were very kindly received by Captain Drew, the superintendent of the station, as well as by his family, with whom we took up our quarters. Captain Drew, after we had taken some refreshment, showed us over the station. He has upwards of five hundred prisoners under his charge, a large proportion of whom are either suffering from disease or are infirm, and not able to work, this being what is called an invalid station, to which they are sent from other places in the colony. The establishment appeared to us to be under good discipline throughout, and such as was calculated to conduce as much to the comfort of the inmates as is consistent with their safe keeping. We were shown the remains of a small skiff which three of the men had constructed in the bush by stealth, and which was made of sticks and thick bark, in which they had endeavoured to make their escape a few days since; but in consequence of its being upset soon after it left the shore, they were thrown into the water, and were obliged to swim back to land, where they were soon taken, and are now awaiting their trial for the offence. * *

"12th mo. 24th.—This morning distributed tracts to the able-bodied prisoners, or effectives, as they are designated by the officers of the establishment, which seemed to be the completion of the little service required of us at Impression Bay; and after breakfast we took leave of our kind host Captain Drew, who supplied us with a couple of horses and a prisoner for a guide for about seven miles through the bush, where we reached a tramroad, on which we travelled five miles more in a small vehicle which held ourselves and our luggage, pushed along by four men at the rate of about four miles an hour, except going down some pretty steep hills, when the poor men jumped up on the side of the carriage, and its own weight impelled us on at a much greater rate than felt quite pleasant; but, through the protection of Providence, we arrived at a boat station at the head of

Long Bay, where we were met by a whale boat rowed by four men, and reached Port Arthur soon after one o'clock, where we met with a cordial reception from James Boyd, the newly-appointed commandant. Port Arthur is beautifully situated at the head of a small bay, and, from the number of buildings, has the appearance of a small town more than of a penal settlement. After dinner, James Boyd showed us over the station, and it was very interesting to see many of the men steadily employed at various trades—carpenters, blacksmiths, ironfounders, harness makers, tailors, and shoemakers were all cheerfully engaged at their callings in different workshops, with no more apparent restraint than free men. But to our horror, I think I may say, a very different scene soon met our eye—as many as fifty or sixty men returning from their work at the stone quarries, all heavily ironed with chains on their legs, some weighing probably thirty pounds or more, attended by their overseers, and followed by two constables with loaded muskets on their shoulders. Before going into their quarters they were arranged in two rows, and each underwent a strict search by the officers to see that they had nothing concealed about their persons that they might use in making their escape, or freeing themselves from their chains; and we were told they underwent this examination every night, many of them being desperate characters, who have been convicted again and again of heinous crimes, and have been proved not fit, for the safety of society, to be entrusted with more liberty. Yet even to these the door of hope is by no means shut. When they give satisfactory evidence of a desire to amend, and a willingness to submit to the needful discipline of the establishment in its milder forms, their burdens are lightened, and every encouragement is held out to them to persevere. * * going freely amongst them, it was painful to see so much of a disposition prevalent to make out that they were either sent there wrongfully or for very trifling offences, when many of them, we cannot doubt, were stained with

crimes of the deepest dye. We endeavoured in a kind
and friendly manner to turn their minds in a different
direction; but it was very distressing to find so little
sense of their true condition as there was manifested
among them.

"Third day, 27th.—During the day we visited the
remainder of the prisoners under separate treatment,
twenty-two in number, eleven of whom were suffering
solitary confinement, in cells perfectly dark, on an allow-
ance of bread and water. This is felt to be a dreadful
punishment, and under no circumstances exceeds thirty
days at one time, the most hardened criminals generally
being subdued before this period is expired. We had
some very interesting interviews. Two desperate characters, who had been sent out to this colony when very
young—mere boys—and since that time had been re-
sentenced to Norfolk Island, from whence they had been
recently returned, were of this class. One of them was a
remarkable character. He had been out in the bush for
a length of time, and had subsisted by robbery and plun-
der; but, as he told us, his hands had never been stained
with the blood of his fellow-man, though he had been
guilty of every other crime. He was a powerful, athletic
man, with an eye of fire, and of iron sinew—formed for a
leader, and had been the terror of those around him; but
his heart was not steeled against the kindlier sympathies
of our nature; and before we parted the tears rolled down
his cheeks, and he acknowledged his thankfulness for our
visit.

"Many who at first looked strangely upon us, and
seemed at a loss to understand our motives in wishing to
see them, were softened before we left them, some saying
that they had not been accustomed to see any one who
could feel for them, and warmly expressing their gratitude
for our kindly notice. On our recommending to one of
those who had recently come up from Norfolk Island to
think on serious things, he gave us to understand that

religion was something which had not been thought of
by either bond or free at that place; and from the account others gave us, it appears to have been a dreadful
place, what if I say in some degree like a hell upon
earth, where, instead of helping and feeling one for
another, the prisoners, as well as many of those set over
them, took a fiendish pleasure in tormenting each other.

"12th mo. 29th.—Last evening we took a walk over
the settlement with the superintendent, and up through
a beautiful valley, in which there are the largest quantity
of tree ferns we have seen, and of a great size. The
stems of many of them are from half a yard to two feet
in diameter, and the leaves upwards of twelve feet in
length. It might truly be called a valley of ferns, as for
a distance of half a mile or upwards there was not much
of anything else. * * * Eagle Hawk Neck is a narrow
strip of land two or three hundred yards wide, which
connects Tasman's Peninsula with the mainland. A
military guard of thirty soldiers, and a number of constables are stationed here to prevent the escape of any
of the convicts from the peninsula. A cordon of seventeen large and savage-looking dogs are chained at short
distances across the Neck, and between each dog is a
post to which a lamp is attached, which is lighted at
night, so that it would seem impossible for any one to
pass unnoticed, particularly as the dogs, on the approach
of any stranger even at a distance, set up a furious noise
and spring from their lairs as if they would devour any
one coming within their reach. But so strong is the
desire for liberty that the poor prisoners do sometimes
try to get past this formidable guard by swimming across
the narrow arm of the sea below the Neck during the
night; but as constables are stationed all along the
coast, it is not often that they are able to get away, and
when brought back they are very severely punished. * *
"Previous to leaving the Cascade Station I did not feel
easy without having a private opportunity of conversing

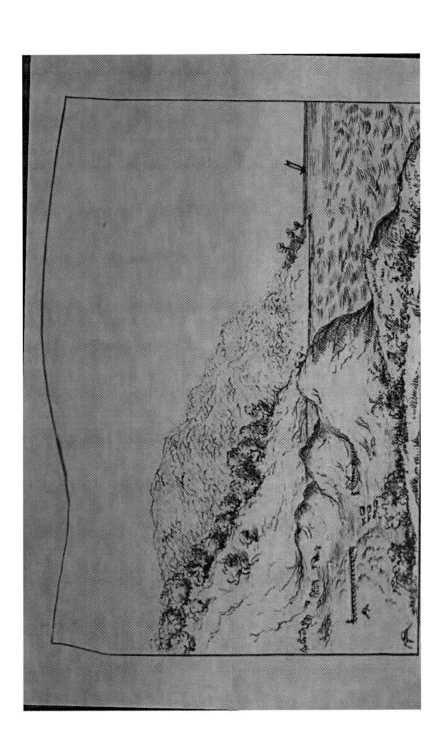

with two men in separate cells who had been troublesome
characters, and were then undergoing six months solitary
confinement, heavily chained, for a violent assault upon
one of the overseers. One of them was transported when
only a boy; has been a very unruly character, and been
convicted of serious crimes since coming here, so that
he has rarely been out of punishment. He told me this
morning to my horror, that previous to our visiting him
he had made up his mind, when he got out of solitary
confinement, to procure a knife and murder some one, in
order that he might be brought to the gallows; but he
said, that seeing the interest we had taken in his welfare he had now given up the intention, and hoped to
be able to redeem his character. I encouraged him to
write to us when he got through his present sentence,
which would expire in about five months, which he agreed
to do, and let us know his future prospects. Poor man!
I fear for him, lest after all his good resolutions should
prove to be written as in the sand, which the first wave
of temptation may be sufficient to sweep away.

" First day, 1st mo. 1st, 1854.— * * * We have now
visited all the stations on the Peninsula, on which there
are altogether about seventeen hundred prisoners and
probably three hundred free persons, including officers of
every kind and their families. It may be said to be one
great prison, and no individual, though free, after having
landed on it, is allowed to leave without permission from
the magistrate. It has been a place of deep though
painful interest to us, and thankful am I in feeling a
peaceful release granted in the prospect of returning to
Hobart Town. But long will the hours I have spent with
the poor outcasts confined here be brought to my remembrance: deep have been and are my sympathies for them.
I have been enabled to place my soul as in their soul's
stead, and have seen that their bondage is bitter, being
bound in affliction and iron, not only bodily but also
spiritually; and earnest have been my prayers that the

Lord would be pleased to break their bonds and set their
captive spirits free from the thraldom of sin and Satan,
snatch some of them as brands from the burning, and
bring them into the glorious liberty of the sons of God for
His mercy's sake."

R. L. held religious meetings with most of the prisoners at their several establishments, and gave them
tracts. On returning to Hobart Town, the visiting magistrate put a letter into my father's hand, expressing his
warm approval of the object of their visit, and his earnest
desire that their labours might be blessed.

R. L. and F. M., with G. W. Walker, called upon
the Lieutenant-Governor and the Comptroller-General,
who wished to know the opinion they had formed of the
management and treatment of the prisoners, and also
if they had any suggestions to make, when they were
glad to have the opportunity of mentioning a few things
they had noticed which seemed to require alteration,
which remarks were kindly received, and they were
assured that they would be attended to.

Wishing to visit some settlers about forty miles from
Hobart Town, my father and his companion set out with
a guide; but owing to the bush fires they had to return.
The journal says:—

"We came in sight of some bush fires, and in the distance before us saw dense clouds of smoke rising into the
air in the direction we had to go; but still we hoped we
might be able to make our way past them, until we came
to a place where we were surrounded on every side except
the way we had come. We rode up on to an eminence
to see if there was any possibility of proceeding, and
behold! the smoke of the country went up like the smoke

of a furnace, and the heat from the fires, although the main body of it was still at some distance, was sufficient to make it evident that any attempt to go forward would be very imprudent, and at the risk of the lives of both man and beast; so, after calmly deliberating, we concluded to return, in doing which we found that some small fires we had passed two hours before had spread so rapidly as to make it very hot work to pass them, and in some places we had to go between the flames, burning furiously on each side of the road, which was nothing more than a bridle path through the bush. Before we had gone far, the clouds began to gather blackness, and in a short time the thunder was pealing amongst the hills. The artillery of heaven and the lightning's flash, added to the dense clouds of smoke arising on every side from burning bush, formed altogether a spectacle the most fearfully sublime that I had ever witnessed. This was succeeded by a heavy shower, which drenched us to the skin, and would contribute in some degree to stop the progress of the fires."

Our travellers now left Hobart Town and proceeded to Melbourne. On arriving there, after speaking of the city, and its streets and houses, my father says:—

"But the dust is what I think I should find it very difficult to become reconciled to. It may be said, in conjunction with the excessive drought, to spoil everything. Flies are another very great annoyance, and they are so persevering in their endeavours to locate themselves on any part of the person that is exposed to their attacks, particularly the head and face, that it is no little work to keep driving them off."

R. L. visited all the Friends, and those connected with them, in Melbourne and the neighbourhood. A Monthly Meeting was established during their stay.

" Third day, 21st.—My mind this day or two past has
been led to look back more than usual to my dear wife
and family, and to the many home endearments with
which a merciful and gracious Providence has seen meet
to bless one who was altogether unworthy of the least of
His mercies. Oh! how these tender ties cling around
the heart of the husband and the father! The Lord only
knows the closeness of the trial it is to my nature to bear
the continued separation from the bosom of a tenderly
beloved wife and dear children. * * Surely nothing less
than that Almighty grace to which all things are possible
could have sustained me under the trial hitherto; and,
though my heart is sometimes ready to sink within me
when I consider how oft the moon may wax and wane,
how oft the sun may rise and set, before I shall be permitted to behold the faces of those loved ones, and of her,
dear above all, whose cherished image is present with me
by night and by day, why should I distrust the power of
Him who hath supported me thus far to do it even unto
the end?

" 4th mo. 25th.—This morning we were cheered by a
bright sky, and pleasant prospect of the land, as we
steamed and sailed up to Port Adelaide, which we were
favoured to enter about nine o'clock. * *

" 28th.—Went to look over the meeting-house premises in North Adelaide. The building is of wood, and
was sent out from England twelve or fourteen years ago.
It is well suited for the purpose, and will conveniently
accommodate at least a hundred persons.

" 5th mo. 3rd.—This morning we left Adelaide in company with our friend Joseph May, and came on to his
residence at Mount Barker. I drove in a spring cart along
with him, and Frederic rode on horseback. * * About five
miles from Adelaide we entered on a range of grassy hills
pretty well timbered, which continued to within four or

five miles of Mount Barker, which is twenty-two miles from Adelaide, when the country became more open, though still partially wooded, mostly with the gum trees, the white stems of which, contrasted with the dark green foliage, have a striking effect.

"5th mo. 12th.— * * * The last few cold days have very much cleared the leaves off the vines in our friend Joseph May's garden, and the few grapes that are left are very much losing their flavour. But it has been a great treat both to Frederic and myself to have the privilege of helping ourselves in any quantity to this pleasant and wholesome fruit, of which our friends here have a most abundant supply, this climate being very favourable for the growth of the vine."

Having visited the families and individuals connected with Friends in South Australia, my father returned to Sydney, and from thence went to Melbourne again, and spent two weeks in the neighbourhood of the gold diggings, wishing to meet with some parties who, they had been told, were there. They next visited Western Australia, where only one member of the Society of Friends resided, and set sail from thence for Cape Town, South Africa. While at the diggings, my father relates a rather disagreeable incident which occurred to them.

"First day, 17th.—After breakfast walked out to distribute a few tracts, when we unexpectedly fell into what I can compare to nothing less than a hornet's nest. Inadvertently and unknowingly we offered a couple of tracts at the house of the Catholic priest, who came out and abused us in the most scurrilous manner, seeming almost maddened with rage, calling out to some men who were with him to horsewhip us, which one of them did, the priest meanwhile threatening to knock our heads together

if we did not take ourselves away, although we were not
on his premises, but on the open unenclosed land. They
laid violent hands on us repeatedly ; and had not one of
their own party more moderate than the rest restrained
them, I do not know to what lengths they would have
proceeded, there being no one near to witness the outrage
but their own party. Neither the priest nor his company
would hear a word we had to say, but ran upon us with
one accord as if we had been wild beasts. Through the
Lord's preserving care we received no harm ; but sorrowful was it to see such a sample of bigotry and intolerance
in one professing to be a minister of Christ, as well as
the blind zeal which actuated his followers, showing us
what we might expect if the Romish Church again became dominant.

" Second day, 18th. — * * * On our return to our
quarters we passed the house of the Catholic priest with
whom we had the rencounter yesterday, and feeling desirous of speaking a word to him, now that he had had time
to reflect on his conduct, we stopped at his door and
asked to see him in a friendly way ; which we had no
sooner done than one of two men who were at work
in the yard rushed upon us, and threatened to cleave
our heads with his spade. The fury of his countenance
showed that he lacked nothing of the will to do it. We
tried to quiet him, but all in vain ; when the priest came
out, to whom we essayed to say a few words, but all to
no purpose ; when he invited us to follow him into his
yard in the direction of some outbuildings ; but at once
seeing the snare he was laying to get us into his power,
we refused, when he said something to the import,
' Then you are not prepared to become martyrs to your
faith !' And we had good reason to believe that it was
his intention to do us a mischief, if not to take away our
lives. Nevertheless we felt nothing but goodwill in our
hearts towards him, as Frederic told them, and very
painful was it to us to leave them in such an unpleasant

M.W. CLIFTONS RESIDENCE, AUSTRALIND

way; but having done simply what seemed to be our duty, we must endeavour to leave it in the hands of Him who out of seeming evil is able to educe good.

"Australind, Western Australia.— * * * About two o'clock we reached the hospitable abode of Marshall Waller Clifton, which may truly be compared to an oasis in the desert.

"24th.—The weather to-day is again very warm, the thermometer 98° in the shade. Our friends the Cliftons live in a good brick house, and have about them all the comforts and conveniences of life. They have a very large garden well stocked with vines, now in full bearing, figs and melons of various kinds. The soil appears to be little but sand, but by good cultivation it seems to be capable of improvement. Potatoes, onions, and maize grow well here; but the plan of forming a settlement according to the prospectus of a company in London by whom our friend M. W. Clifton was sent out as chief commissioner, has completely failed. Our friend Eleanor Clifton appears to have maintained the consistency of her character as a member of our Society, in the very difficult and singular position in which she is placed, having from conviction adopted the views and practices of Friends, and being the only one professing with them in the colony of Western Australia. She has been in delicate health for a considerable time, but when she has been well enough we understand it has been her practice to go and sit down with such of her family as chose to accompany her on first day mornings in a little meeting house which she brought out with her from England fourteen years ago, and which stands in a nice retired situation at a short distance from their dwelling house. * * *

"In the neighbourhood of Australind we saw more of the natives than we have before fallen in with. I think one morning I counted a dozen in the yard adjoining M. W. Clifton's house. They are inoffensive and peaceable, and many of them of an intelligent and interesting countenance. The Cliftons employ them in miscellaneous work, for which they always pay them in money, or some other way; but they do not like steady employment of any kind. The adults, both male and female, wear a covering of kangaroo skin reaching about to the knees, which is gracefully thrown over the left shoulder and fastened under the right arm, leaving this entirely at liberty. The children up to four or five years of age go entirely naked. Their wants in this climate are very few. They have no fixed habitation of any kind. When night comes they make a fire in the bush and lie down beside it, with a few boughs or a few pieces of bark reared up on the windward side. Their food is the kangaroo, the kangaroo rat, snakes, grubs, fish, and roots, which they find everywhere, and take them as they need. They have no cooking utensils nor chattels of any kind. They are very fond of flour, and procure it from the settlers when they can, and make it into cakes which they bake in the ashes. They have also acquired a taste for tobacco, of which they are very fond.

"3rd mo. 13th, 1855.—On board the barque Devonshire, six days out from Swan River, on her way to England, touching at the Cape of Good Hope.

"4th mo., 2nd.— * * * My mind is pained on this, as on many of our former voyages, in beholding the way in which the poor seamen are treated on board ship, and that want of consideration of their feelings and their comfort displayed towards them by their officers in general. These remarks will too frequently also apply to steerage passengers; and although Captain Dixon is very kind and attentive to his cabin passengers, and probably as much so as is usual to his crew, yet I have mourned over that system of uncontrolled power invested in those having command of vessels at sea, as leading them to look for that servile and abject submission which is inconsistent with the freedom and liberty of man. * * *

LIGHTHOUSE, GREEN POINT, CAPE

" 9th.—Progressing favourably. Our first mate this morning reports that in the middle watch, a little before four o'clock, a large meteor, having the appearance of fifty or one hundred blue lights, passed over the ship from west to east, making the complete arch of the heavens to within twenty degrees of the horizon, when it disappeared. The time of its passing did not occupy more than two or three seconds, but it left behind it the appearance of a train of fire, which remained visible for about a minute. He says he was sensible of a great heat whilst it was passing, and both he and others who saw it describe it as producing the light of noon day.

" 4th mo. 21st.—Still on the L'Agulhas Bank, unable to attain to our desired haven, the wind having been directly in our teeth for the last eight days, so that although we have been tacking the whole of the time we have been barely able to maintain our position.

" 23rd.—On going on deck this morning found that our vessel was standing off land, a dense fog having come on which rendered it unsafe for us to stand in ; but as the day advanced it cleared away, and enabled us to see the land from which we were distant eight or ten miles. The wind however was contrary, and we had to tack backwards and forwards some hours before we were able to make Table Bay, which we fortunately did about three this afternoon, and came to an anchor about five.

" Cape Town, South Africa, 24th.—This forenoon, after some delay in waiting for a boat, we succeeded in landing our luggage, and through the kind assistance of an individual to whom Captain Dixon kindly introduced us, we pretty soon were located in comfortable lodgings with a Dutch family of the name of Hout. After fixing upon our quarters we went to enquire for our letters at H. E. Rutherford and Brothers, to whose care we had directed our letters to be forwarded. We found one each

from England. * * * From the little we have seen of
Cape Town, it is the most foreign-looking place we have
seen in the colonies. The houses and the people are
altogether un-English. It is a thoroughly Dutch town
inhabited by all nations. Table Mountain, at the foot of
which the place is built, is a singular looking mass of
rocks about three thousand feet in height. The Bay is
very open and exposed to the north-west winds, which
sometimes blow very hard and endanger the shipping.

" 27th.— * * * In the afternoon visited the Friends'
School in Buiten Street for coloured children under the
care of Mary Jennings and daughters. There were upwards of one hundred present, the greater part of them
Malays. Some of them could read tolerably, and several
of them were learning to write. Considering the wild
and untutored race to which they belong, M. J.'s labours
appear to have had a favourable effect, and the liberality
of Friends in England in founding and supporting such a
school may, I hope, be as bread cast upon the waters,
which may be found after many days.

" 5th mo. 2nd.—Made a short call upon the Governor,
Sir George Grey, whom we had previously seen in New
Zealand, when he was governor of that colony. He
received us in a free and friendly manner, and on our
taking leave of him very kindly enquired if there was
anything he could do for us.

" 5th mo. 16th.—This day I complete my fifty-fourth
year. Of my ten last birthdays only one has been passed
in England, nine of them have been on a foreign shore;
one in Ireland, five in America, and three in the
Southern Hemisphere.

" Fifth day, 17th.—Our favourable wind of yesterday
held on through the night, and at daylight this morning
we entered Algoa Bay, very little more than an open

CAPE TOWN, S.A.

A VIEW, IN STRAND ST. 1791

oadstead, being entirely exposed to the south-easters,
which sometimes blow here with great fury and do much
damage to the shipping. The surf, even in moderate
weather, breaks with considerable violence. The boats
which came off to take us on shore were large, and had
each five men, four to row and one at the stern oar. As
soon as the boat touched the shore we were surrounded
by a number of Coolies, who seized our luggage and offered their backs to carry us through the water to dry
land, of which we were glad to avail ourselves. The
boat, on account of the shallowness of the water, being
unable to come nearer than within several yards. It
was an amusing sight to see the Coolies dash into the
water as we approached the shore, and when they have
performed their momentary service they are not at all
backward in claiming their reward. The town of Port
Elizabeth extends for a mile or two along the beach and
contains some good buildings, and appears to be a place
of considerable trade. We were not a little surprised to
see so large a number of drays in the street with from
twelve to sixteen bullocks each, which bring produce from
the interior and take back supplies. * * *

" 18th, Port Elizabeth.—The Fingoes are a numerous
people here, and appear to be usefully employed in loading
and unloading the vessels. We observed numbers of them
on the beach this morning carrying goods through the
surf on their shoulders, most of them in a state of nudity;
fine well-formed men of great muscular power, and work-
ing very cheerfully under the superintendence of a white
man. The appearance of the place however is decidedly
more English than Cape Town, both as regards the buildings and the inhabitants, at least the white portion of
them. Very little of the Dutch character, so prevalent
in Cape Town, is to be observed here. This afternoon at
two o'clock left Port Elizabeth by omnibus for Uitenhage,
where we had heard of two or three individuals who had
had some connection with Friends.

I

" 5th mo. 20th.— * * * It is sorrowful to find in the short time we have been in the colony such a spirit of war and bloodshed pervading the minds of the settlers as is manifestly the case, consequent in a great degree upon the incursions of the Kaffirs, towards whom there appears to exist a feeling of the deepest animosity, most painfully inconsistent with the conduct which a people professing the benign principles of Christianity are called upon to show forth to these uncivilized and barbarous people.

" 22nd.—On renewing our enquiries this morning after a conveyance to Graham's Town, we learnt that there were some parties just come down from the interior and intending to leave again this afternoon, with whom we agreed to go as far as Graham's Town, one of the wag- gons being a covered one, in which they thought they could accommodate us. The time was short in which we had to prepare for the journey; but by the assistance of an individual who kindly interested himself about us were able to get the necessary stores, and to be ready for the waggon which started between twelve and one. We were three drays in company, fourteen bullocks in each, two Englishmen, the proprietors of the waggons, and five coloured drivers and leaders, two of them Kaffirs and three of them Fingoes or Hottentots. About eight in the evening we outspanned on the edge of a Salt Pan across the Swort Kops River. Here we had our first experience of South African bush camping. Our Kaffirs and Fingoes kindled a fire, at which we boiled our kettle and cooked our meal for our supper, and afterwards stretched our- selves upon our boxes in the bottom of our waggon, where we got a moderate night's rest, with the exception of the wet coming in through the cover of our vehicle, the rain falling very heavily for some hours. Soon after crossing the Swort Kops River we had the misfortune to be overturned; and a great mercy it was that neither of us sustained the slightest injury, although our boxes and luggage were thrown upon us with some force. By

TRAVELLING TO GRAHAM'S TOWN, S. AFRICA –

all putting our shoulders to the wheel we were enabled to
get the waggon up and resume our journey; thankful, I
may truly say, to that ever-watchful Eye which had preserved us from harm in the accident, which appears to
have arisen from the carelessness of our driver.

" 23rd.—There had been so much rain in the night,
and the ground was so wet, that our men were in no
haste to be moving; and the grass and sticks were so
soaked with rain that it required a little patience before
even our Kaffirs could get the fire to burn to boil the
kettle. Understanding from the proprietors of the waggon that they were intending to take a loading of salt
from here, we concluded to call upon the owner of the
Salt Pan, an old Dutchman, whose house was in sight,
where we met a very hospitable reception and a pressing
invitation to take breakfast, which we were not backward
to do, much preferring it to cooking for ourselves in the
bush, more particularly as our box of provisions, bread,
butter, cheese, coffee, tea, sugar, &c., by our last night's
overthrow had been pretty much mixed up together, also
a number of eggs with which we had provided ourselves
smashed amongst them. The loading of the three
waggons occupied our men most of the day, and our hospitable Dutchman would not be satisfied unless we went
to dine with him. * * * The Salt Pan, near which we
outspanned last night, is a sheet of shallow water two or
three miles in circumference, similar to one or two others
we have seen in the neighbourhood of Algoa Bay, from
which large quantities of salt are annually collected by
men who go into the water and simply scrape it from
the bottom, which to some extent appears to be a solid
layer of beautiful white salt.

" 25th.—The past night was very cold, and the ground
this morning covered with hoar frost, but having plenty
of covering we managed to keep ourselves tolerably warm
and slept well. Our men laid around the fire on the

ground covered with their karosses, where they seemed
quite at home. At sunrise they roused up to prepare
their breakfasts, some of them kindly assisting us also,
which I found them very willing to do after presenting
each of the Kaffirs and Fingoes with a threepenny piece,
with which they seemed much pleased. At noon we
outspanned on a grassy plain, and on searching for the
watering place found it to be a muddy stagnant pond,
partly covered with a green scum, but of which we were
glad to drink, there being no choice, and also to fill our
kettles; though to our surprise when some of the oxen
came to it to drink they turned away.

" 26th.—This morning moved on before sunrise, and
about nine o'clock outspanned near Riet Vley, and there
being a house of accommodation a little off the road, my
companion and self took the opportunity of having a
shave and a good wash, which we had not been able to
have for two or three days. Here also we got our bottle
filled with milk at the hut of a Fingoe hard by, who had
a numerous flock of goats and several cows. These huts
were of the rudest construction, something of the shape
of a beehive, and formed of reeds or straw and sticks.
The children were running about in a state of nudity,
with the exception of a small fringed belt a few inches
square fastened by a string round their loins. The
women wore a little more clothing; but some of these
were without any covering on the upper part of their
bodies. The men were clad after the manner of the
whites. We noticed in each of the two huts into which
we looked at least two females, who I took to be the
wives of the two Fingoe men whom we saw about the
cattle kraal, which was nothing more than a rude en-
closure of sticks and bushes, into which they drive the
cattle at night. Both the Fingoes and Kaffirs allow of a
plurality of wives, whom they purchase and pay for generally with cattle.* * * The owner of the waggon in which
we travel had been actively engaged in the late Kaffir

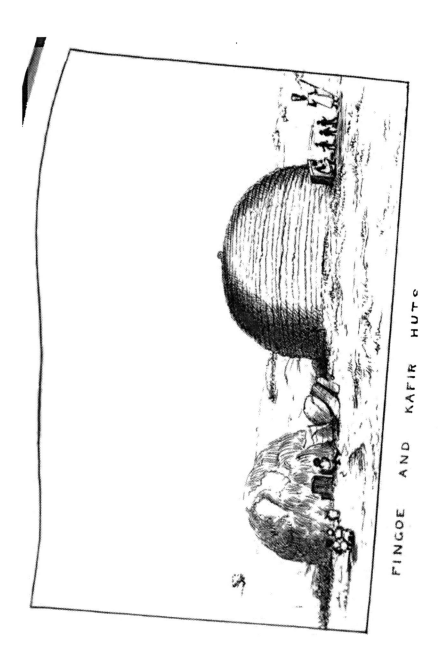

FINGOE AND KAFIR HUTc

war, and had suffered deeply from their incursions and
depredations upon his property; and in speaking of the
warfare carried on against them by the whites, I was
pained to hear him tell of having himself shot down as
many as seven Kaffirs with as little concern as most of
us would have in shooting a dog. * * * The tendency in
man to go back to barbarism, even after having had every
advantage from civilized society, has often struck me
when coming into close contact with those who have
emigrated from Europe, and become from surrounding
circumstances associated with the native tribes. This
is very evident in the owner of the waggon in which we
are now travelling. He came out from Devonshire about
twelve years ago, and has from his occupation mixed
continually with the natives, and now, when camping
out, he sits down at the bush fire, and with the excep-·
tion of his dress, seems like one of them, conversing
with them in their own language and evidently enjoying
their society. There are however exceptions, and we
occasionally fall in with those who have withstood this
tendency, and after much exposure still retain their relish
for the refined habits of civilized and cultivated society.

"Schiet Kop, First day, 5th mo. 27th, 1855.—* * *
Fell in with a Kaffir family, consisting of an elderly female, the mother, her son and his wife, with three young
children, and a young woman, sister to the married man.
The man could understand a little English, and was very
ready to show us into their hut, which was of a beehive
shape, made of reeds and sticks, with a low opening on
one side, which served both as the door and chimney.
The arms and legs of the females were ornamented with
brass rings, and both they and the children had necklaces
of the teeth of the wild cat. On leaving them I presented the man with a silver threepenny piece, on which
he got up, and, before I was at all aware of what he was
going to do, stooped down to the earth and kissed my
shoe.

"28th.— * * To-day we were four waggons in company, making a pretty long train, fourteen bullocks to each waggon. The driver's whip has a handle of bamboo cane, twelve or thirteen feet in length, with a still longer lash of bullock's hide, with which he urges on his team, and which, when he cracks, makes a report so loud as to be heard at a great distance. One of the whips I measured, including the handle and lash, was thirty-two feet; but this, long as it is, does not enable the driver, when sitting on the front of his waggon, to reach more than half the length of his team.

"Graham's Town, South Africa, 6th mo. 1st.—* * * Took a walk out of town to the villages of the natives, located on a tract of land appropriated to their use, none of them being allowed to live in the town. The Hottentots appear to be the lowest in the scale of improvement, at least as far as regards their dwellings, their huts in general being the meanest places we can conceive, though they have adopted the practice of clothing themselves after the manner of the whites much more than the Kaffirs and Fingoes. The dwellings of the two latter are, however, very superior, and they appear to have more thrift and management about them than the poor Hottentots.

"6th mo. 7th.—Called upon several parties with whom we had made acquaintance, one of these an elderly man from near Halifax, who came out with the first settlers to Algoa Bay in 1820. He had succeeded tolerably well, and had a fine flock of fifteen hundred sheep, and a number of cattle on his farm, all of which he lost from the incursions of the Kaffirs, and is now in reduced circumstances; but a bright example of Christian resignation under all. He is in connection with the Wesleyans, and is much esteemed amongst them. In speaking of an occasion wherein he, with others, was called upon by the magistrate to hold himself in readiness to go and fight

BAIN'S KLOOF — S. AFRICA.

the Kaffirs, he told them that 'he did not feel comfortable, after going down upon his knees to pray for the
Kaffir, to go and shoot him.' Would to God that many
others had felt so likewise, and had shown forth to those
uncivilized tribes an example of Christian forbearance
consistent with the principles of Him whose followers
they profess themselves to be!

"8th.— * * Took tea at George Impey's. * * His
son William is a Wesleyan minister, married and settled
in Graham's Town. He was present, and we had some
interesting conversation on important subjects. But it
has been very sorrowful to my mind, since coming into
South Africa, to find the pious and influential part of the
religious community, with very little exception, endeavouring to justify the warlike measures pursued towards the
native tribes of this country, instead of inculcating by
precept and example the benign and peaceable doctrines
of Him who came not to destroy men's lives, but to save
them.

"12th.—Left Jackson's about seven, and travelled on
twenty miles over a hilly and rough mountainous district,
and outspanned for two hours on a grassy plain, where
there was a little feed for our horses. As soon as we
stopped, Frederic and myself set out to seek the watering
place which we had been given to understand was near.
After some search, we found a hole of muddy water, which
reminded me of the drainage of a farm yard, which we
could scarcely believe was the water we were told of.
But on our driver coming to it, he pronounced it, to our
surprise, to be excellent; and, on our hinting that it did
not seem very nice to make our coffee from, he remarked
that being thick with mud would answer instead of milk,
of which we had none. When the kettle boiled, we made
our coffee and sat down to our frugal meal, all of us agree-
ing that, notwithstanding the water was thickened with
mud, the coffee was excellent, a good appetite taking

away all our squeamishness about the dirty water. * * *
On making some enquiry about the means of getting
forward to Wheatlands, the residence of our friend Emma
Parkes and family, we learnt that on account of the horse
sickness having been very fatal in this neighbourhood, it
would be in vain to think of getting a conveyance here,
and that our only chance was to agree with the man who
brought us up from Graham's Town to go on with us. * *
From Graham's Town to Somerset there may be said to
be no road. It is merely a track which is made by the
bullock waggons, nothing whatever having been done in
the way of levelling or filling up, and it was marvellous
to me that our vehicle was not broken to pieces in going
through the rocky ravines and drifts so frequently met
with. The aspect of the country was barren in the ex-
treme, not a single tree of any size to be seen, but here
and there low shrubs of different kinds peculiar to this
climate, amongst which the aloe was very conspicuous,
and being generally in flower it had a very pretty appearance. In one part we passed through swarms of locusts
for some miles together, which cause great destruction to
vegetation wherever they come; but happily they are
migratory, and pass in masses from one part to another,
and do not stay long in one locality. They are a large
brown insect, from one to two inches in length. They
were very numerous on the ground, whilst large numbers
were flying through the air in various directions. * *

"The distances in this part of South Africa are computed by hours, and not by miles, supposing a horseman
well mounted to make from six to seven miles an hour.
On enquiring how far it is to such and such a place, we
should be answered, it is five or seven hours, as the case
might be. Jackals and wolves are not uncommon in
these parts. * * We got sight of a small herd of spring-
boks; but they did not allow us to come very near them,
and quickly took fright on seeing us approach the place
where they were feeding. Soon after three o'clock we
reached Wheatlands, and found to our regret that our

Friend Emma Parkes had left that morning for Uitenhage, having been sent for by her husband, who was somewhat indisposed. We were, however, very kindly received by her children, four sons and two daughters, most of whom are grown up. Their establishment is about the most complete that we have seen. The buildings are good, in the old Dutch style, with all needful conveniences. There is a vineyard of considerable extent, from which they make annually a large quantity of wine and brandy; about fifty acres of land in cultivation, and several thousand acres of 'karroo,' which supports two or three flocks of sheep and goats. The 'karroo' is a low shrub, a few inches in height, having very much the appearance of thyme, and to an observer seems to have no goodness in it; but the sheep which are accustomed to it thrive upon it, and appear in excellent condition.

" Sixth day, 29th, Port Elizabeth.—On our return to town to-day, received a letter from our invalid friend Alfred Gilpin, dated Cape Town, giving account of his increased weakness, and of the probability that he could not hold out very long, yet thinking it possible that he might see us once more, desiring at the same time to be resigned to the Lord's will, whatever it might be.

" 7th mo. 20th.—On drawing near Cape Town, we met many waggons returning into the country, having come in with produce of various kinds. Some were drawn by oxen, and some of the lighter vehicles by mules—six, eight, and ten in each. The omnibus by which we went up to Paarl had eight horses in it, and one of the stages, I noticed, we had ten; and these are all guided by one man, who sits on the box, and reins these ten horses with as much ease and precision as our first-rate English coachmen would four. Another man sits at his side with a whip at least thirty feet in length, which he uses when he sees it needed. But to see a man driving away with ten in hand would, I have thought, shame some of our

English drivers, who pride themselves upon being able to drive four. * * * We have been very much struck, on entering into conversation with the missionaries whom we have fallen in with in South Africa, respecting the treatment of the native tribes by the British Government and the settlers, to hear such very contrary accounts from those connected with the Wesleyans and the London Missionary Society—the former, with little exception, laying the blame of the disturbances that have arisen on the poor natives; and the latter exonerating them from all blame, and charging it to the unfair dealing of the British Government, or rather on those who have pretended to act under her authority. These conflicting accounts make it exceedingly difficult to come at anything like a decided judgment in the case; but we have been unable to come to the conclusion, from what we have seen and heard, that the whites have at all times acted up to the standard of the golden rule in dealing with the aborigines of South Africa.

"Simon's Town, 8th mo. 1st.—In the afternoon again went out to distribute tracts. On calling at the cottages of many of the coloured people, were surprised to find that many of them could read English, and in some instances those who could not read themselves were desirous to have a tract, saying they could get some one to read it for them. We also got access to the jail, in which were eighteen or twenty prisoners, and left tracts there. The jailor very kindly showed us into the various cells, and the establishment generally appeared to be under good management.

"Cape Town, 8th mo. 2nd.— * * * Soon after we got in went on to see our friend Alfred Gilpin. * * Dr. Abercrombie, who has kindly attended him from the first, thinks he cannot last many days. He is fully aware of his position, and spoke to me to-day respecting some arrangements which would be needful in case of his

MARKET SQUARE, DURBAN, NATAL.

decease. Matilda Simey sat up with him last night, as the doctor says he should not be left, and Frederic Mackie has agreed to take her place to-night.

"Cape Town, 8th mo. 9th, 1855.—Between three and four o'clock attended at Thomas Simey's, where we met from twenty to thirty persons collected to follow the remains of our dear young friend Alfred Gilpin to the grave. Among these were two or three Wesleyan ministers, the minister of the Scotch Church, and of the Independent congregation, and several other pious and influential individuals of the town and neighbourhood, with whom A. G. had become acquainted, and who had manifested a kind Christian interest in his welfare, and had contributed by their sympathy and active attention to his comfort during the time his lot had been cast amongst them. And a blessing I cannot doubt will rest upon them, rendered as I believe it has been unto him as unto one of those respecting whom our Saviour was graciously pleased to say, 'Inasmuch as ye have done it unto one of the least of these, ye have done it unto me.'

"Durban, Port Natal, 9th mo. 14th.— * * This evening we have been making some enquiry after the best means of getting to Pieter Maritzburg, about fifty miles from Durban, in which neighbourhood there are two or three individuals whom we are desirous to see, and find that the only way open for us, or at least the most eligible, will be for us to hire a bullock waggon for the purpose, which we have done, and think of starting tomorrow. * * * This is a place for wild beasts of almost every description, and serpents of various kinds are numerous. Our friend Ralph Clarence was giving us an account of his falling in with a boa constrictor at a short distance from his house, and others have been found in the same neighbourhood of a large size.

"First day, 16th.—We moved forward, and about nine o'clock outspanned on Fields' Hill. Here we cooked our

breakfast from provisions we had taken with us. Here
also a few yards from our waggon we found a snake
between three and four feet long apparently fresh killed,
which a person from the adjoining farm, who came up to
us whilst we were camping, told us was a puff adder, one
of the most deadly kind of serpents in the colony. The
same individual also informed us that about six months
ago a large lion was shot on his farm, which had a short
time previously killed one of his horses.

"Third day, 25th, Ladysmith, Klip River District,
Natal.—Last evening our friend James Mullet took tea
with us at our inn. Since coming out from England he
has, in common with others, seen many changes; and
although his lot has been a secluded one as regards intercourse with such as would have been a strength to him
in the way of the cross, yet it was comforting to believe
that he still retains a warm attachment to the principles
of Friends; and it was pleasant to find that there was an
ear open to receive the word of Christian counsel which
my dear companion and myself each had to hand to
him in the fresh flowings of Gospel love, which had constrained us to undertake a journey of upwards of one
hundred miles through a wilderness country in order to
discharge this debt of love towards our dear friend. * *
In the forenoon called upon the rest of the families in
Ladysmith, and left tracts with them; which having done,
another subject which had claimed my attention came
more weightily before me, and this was the propriety of
holding a meeting for worship in the village, if way should
open for it. * * * In the afternoon a violent thunder-
storm came on, with heavy rain, which continued into the
evening, and seemed likely to prevent the people getting
out, as the colonists here never think of going out in the
rain. Providentially, however, a little before seven o'clock
the rain ceased for a short time, and from twenty to thirty
persons assembled, and through best Help it proved an
open and relieving time. * *

FALL OF THE UMGENI — NATAL — 272 / HIGH

"Yesterday I had a very narrow escape from serious injury, if not from death itself, by my horse, from the slipperiness of the roads, suddenly coming down, and rolling upon me, so that my companion, who was close behind, seemed fully to expect that I must be seriously hurt. But, marvellous to say, though I was covered with mud from head to foot, and my horse went head over heels, yet neither my horse nor myself sustained the slightest injury that I know of, which I can do no less than ascribe to the merciful providence of my Heavenly Father.

"28th.—A wet uncomfortable morning, with a dense Scotch mist and drizzling rain, in which we rode for three or four hours, when about half-past eleven we reached a stopping place at the Umgeni Falls, where we got some forage for our horses and some refreshment for ourselves. The road crosses the Umgeni River here by a ford, which in dry weather may be passed in safety, although only about a hundred yards above the Falls, where the whole river, by one tremendous pitch of 272 feet, descends into the ravine below. But now, owing to the late rains, it was impassable, and we had to make a circuit of three or four miles in order to cross by a wooden bridge which has been erected higher up the river, and in reaching which we had to pass over one or two small streams and some wet swampy ground, which we had great difficulty in getting through. Whilst the woman of the house where we had stopped was preparing us some refreshment, our guide walked down with us to the Falls, which, owing to the river being full, presented a magnificent spectacle. I do not possess the powers of graphic description, so must content myself with saying that next to Niagara it is the grandest that I have ever seen.

"Maritzburg, 10th mo. 1st, 1855.—This forenoon distributed tracts in the town, which were well received, and our only regret was that we had not a sufficient number

to go through the whole of it.   Afterwards made a call
on Dr. Colenso, the resident Bishop of Natal, who was
very friendly, and pressed us much to go and dine with
him, from which we excused ourselves, having some other
engagements.

   " Sixth day, 12th.—Have been engaged in writing
most of the day, and in reading a little work called ' Ten
Weeks in Natal,' by Dr. Colenso, being an account of his
journeyings through the country on his first coming out,
with his observations upon the condition of the native
tribes, and the state of the white population. It is written
in a pleasing style, and affords a good deal of information,
though some of his remarks and conclusions are not satisfactory to some of the colonists.

   " Seventh day, 13th.—We are expecting to go out this
afternoon to our friend Ralph Clarence's, on the Umgeni,
for the purpose of spending first day with them.   When
there on fourth day they informed us that on a night previously a tiger had taken one of their best dogs from off
the ' stoop' close to the door. His wife, who was up with
one of the children, heard the tiger spring upon the dog,
and gave the alarm to her husband, who was immediately
out with his gun; but the tiger was not to be seen, having been driven away by the other dogs, four in number,
and in his hurry had let fall the one which he had just
seized, and which they found lying dead a few yards distant.   The night we were there they supposed the tiger
was again prowling about, from the barking the dogs kept
up great part of the time; but they are so accustomed
to have wild animals around their premises, that it does
not create much alarm. The children reported having
seen a tiger in the bush only a short distance from the
house in the middle of the afternoon a few days previously,
which it was supposed might be the same which killed
the dog, and which made their mother rather afraid to let
the smaller children go far from the house unprotected,

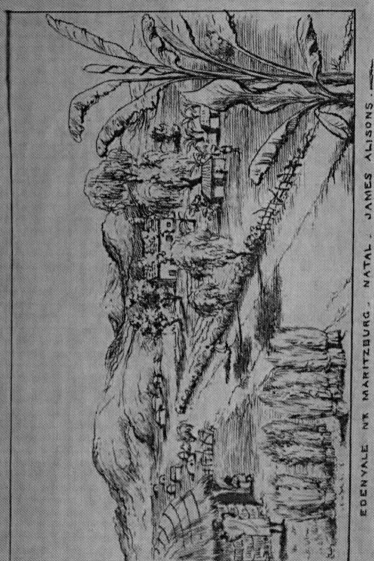

EDENVALE · NR MARITZBURG · NATAL · JAMES ALISONS ·

lest the voracious animal might take a fancy to one of them.

"14th.— * * In the afternoon walked over and took tea at Lucy Spearman's, and had a dark walk back over the hills for about two miles to Ralph Clarence's, not without some fear of falling in with a tiger which has been prowling about their farm for two or three weeks past, and which, before we had been in the house more than an hour, gave evidence of his being near at hand by an attack he made upon the pigsty, and carrying off a fine young pig, which no doubt afforded him a delicious supper. The dogs barked, and the pig squealed, and R. C. and some of his family were quickly out; but all to no purpose. The tiger had got safely into the bush, which was close at hand, and into which even the dogs durst not venture. Before taking the pig, he had got a fowl, which had been put as a bait to lure him into a trap which our friends had set for him, but which from some cause had not gone off.

"15th.—This morning, on our friend R. C. walking out, accompanied by Frederic Mackie, at the distance of three or four hundred yards from the house they came upon the spot where the tiger had made his supper, and where he had also slept for the night, and from which they supposed that their approach had just roused him, and caused him to retire further into the bush. All that was left of the poor pig was one foot, and the entrails, which they are not in the habit of eating, and which are always found left at some little distance from the place where the tiger devours his prey. * *

"In a small lake not more than four or five miles from Ralph Clarence's, and in sight from his house, he told us, the hippopotamus, or sea-cow, as it is called here, is frequently seen, and that they have sometimes come up in the night and walked round his premises. In the river at the bottom of his farm, during the summer season, alligators also abound, and several persons have lost their lives in crossing the ford, which, although it is quite safe to do in the winter, when the alligators, on account of the shallow water, cannot come up; in the summer, which is here the rainy season, when the rivers are full, it is considered very dangerous for any one to venture to do, for fear of being seized by these reptiles. Elephants likewise have recently been seen in the neighbourhood, but are not now often to be met with. The same may be said of the lion, which appears very much to have retreated from these parts. Serpents of many kinds, from the immense boa constrictor, sixteen or eighteen feet long, down to the smaller species, abound here, the bite of some of which is very dangerous. We have hitherto, I am thankful to say, in our varied wanderings, been preserved from coming upon any, although our friend Ralph Clarence's wife told us this morning that a night or two ago they found one on the floor of their sitting room, and that too of a kind which the Kaffir assured them was very venomous. Not long ago their eldest daughter was opening a drawer to take something out, and put her hand upon one coiled up at the bottom of the drawer. And in many other places they have frequently come upon them, yet happily none of them have been bitten. * *

"Third day, 16th.—Made an interesting visit to the camp on the Durban Flat, where about ninety soldiers of the 45th Regiment are located in 'wattle and dab' barracks, and distributed a few tracts amongst them. * * *

"The Bishop of Natal is raising up a strong feeling here in the minds of many by his endeavour to introduce changes in the manner of conducting the services of the Church which are considered of a Tractarian or Puseyite tendency, and to which many who have been in the habit of attending the Episcopal place of worship are decidedly opposed.

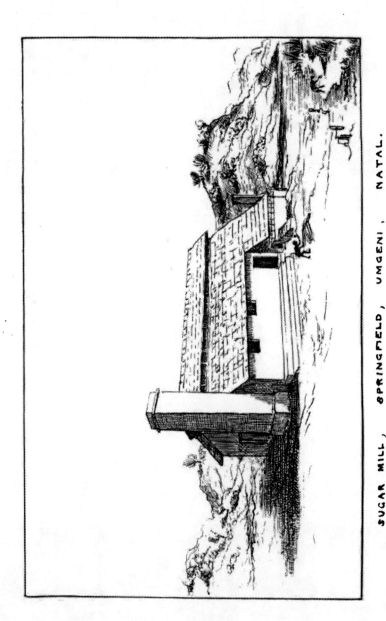

SUGAR MILL, SPRINGFIELD, UMGENI, NATAL.

" Third day, 23rd.—* * * On our returning from the Point this forenoon, we came across a green snake from two to three feet in length, which some one had apparently just killed. It was not thicker than my little finger, and of a bright grass colour, very beautiful to look upon, and not generally considered to be poisonous. The natives, we understand, think that their departed friends after death are turned into green snakes, and on this account they are very careful not to destroy them.

" 10th mo. 24th.— * * * Reached our friend Ralph Clarence's, at the Umgeni, just as they had secured a large tiger or leopard in a strong cage, in which they were going to bring him down in their bullock cart to Durban for sale. He was a very fine animal. From the best sight we could get of him, I should think from the tip of the nose to the end of his tail he was fully eight feet in length. It appears he was caught last night in the trap which R. C. had set for him for a week or ten days past. On finding him there this morning, they at once sent to inform their neighbours, who willingly came and assisted our friend in making a cage and getting him into it, which appears to have been no easy matter. But at length, by means of a strong chain which they got round his neck, and by several of them pulling at it with all their might, they dragged him into the cage, which was only just large enough to admit his body, allowing him to lie down, but scarcely to turn himself over; it not being thought safe to allow him more room for fear he should escape. They suppose it to be the same which has been prowling about R. C.'s for some time, and within the last fortnight has taken a dog, a pig, two fowls, and a hen turkey; a neighbour also charges him with having killed one of his cows; so that there was a general rejoicing at having secured the depredator; although he was by no means pleased with the change;

K

and when any one went very near him, or touched him, he occasionally gave a growl or a roar which made every one look about them very quickly, and soon increase their distance from him.

" Durban, 25th.—Our friend did not meet with a purchaser for his tiger last evening; but this morning I am glad to say he sold him to a person in the town for eight pounds, and we had the pleasure of seeing the noble animal transferred from the small prison in which he had been screwed up for nearly twenty-four hours into a large but strong iron barred cage, where he could fully stretch his limbs ; though by the endeavours he made to free himself from his confinement, he shewed that he would much prefer the liberty of his native kloofs.

" Cape Town, 11th mo. 7th.—* * * I have not yet felt at liberty to make much enquiry about any vessels likely to take my dear companion and myself to our respective destinations, two or three debts of love still remaining on my mind towards some parties in the neighbourhood of Cape Town, which must be discharged before my way feels quite clear to move in engaging passages from here for myself or my companion.

" Cape Town, 11th mo., 1855.—This morning went out by the omnibus to Wynberg, a pleasant village about nine miles from Cape Town. There we hired a cart to take us forward to Constantia, the district famed for producing the best wines in the colony. We called upon two of the largest growers, S. Van Renen and Jacob Cloete, who behaved very courteously, showing us over their extensive premises, altogether in the Dutch style, each of their establishments having been occupied by their ancestors for two or three generations. They have each about forty acres of vineyard, which looked promising

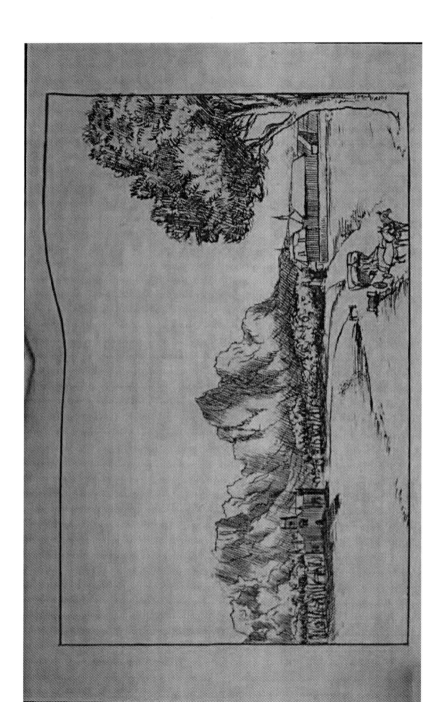

and well. One of them told us that his vineyard sometimes yielded him two hundred casks of wine, of one
hundred and fifty gallons each. We left a few tracts
with each of the families and returned back to Wynberg,
where we distributed a few more, and returned to Cape
Town by the omnibus, having been much pleased with
our little excursion.

" Second day, 12th.—Have felt at liberty this morning
to make enquiry after a vessel to England, and also after
one to Australia for my companion. But though there
are one or more likely to be going in both directions in
the course of the next week or two, we have not yet fixed
upon any. * *

" 13th.—Have this morning been on board the 'John
Knox,' a vessel expected to sail for London in about a
week, and also on board the 'Frederic Huth,' a barque
in the Mauritius trade, by which my dear companion was
thinking of taking his passage, should nothing more
eligible offer, vessels direct from here to Australia being
very rare, and the communication from the Mauritius to
Australia frequent. The 'John Knox' appears to be an
eligible vessel and her accommodations good, and I think
I should be satisfied if the way opens for taking my passage in her.

" 15th.—This morning finally concluded to secure
berths by the two vessels we had under consideration.
* * * No one but the husband who has for years been
separated from the bosom of a tenderly beloved wife, can
understand my feelings in the prospect of shortly being
reunited to her and to our dear children, those sweet
pledges of our long and mutual love. And what adds
infinitely to the pleasantness of the prospect, and without
which all earthly joys are insipid and tasteless, is the
approving smile of our Father who is in Heaven, whose

favour is better than life ; and the feeling of sweet peace
which is mercifully my portion in the winding-up of the
long and arduous service in which my dear companion
and myself have been engaged.

" First day, 18th.— * * * Took tea and spent the
evening at Thomas Simey's, when, to my surprise, I
learned that they had concluded to send their eldest
boy, now nearly fourteen, to England for education, and
that they were intending to take a passage for him by
the ' John Knox,' hoping that I might be able to exercise
a little care over him during the voyage, and see him
safely into the hands of their relatives, who are to take
charge of him in England. I felt it a considerable responsibility, and one from which I would rather have
been excused ; but expressed my willingness to do what
I could in carrying out their wishes.

" 11th mo. 24th.—After an early dinner my dear
companion accompanied me on board the ' John Knox,'
where we found Thomas and Matilda Simey, who had
come off with their son James, who was to be my fellow-
passenger to England. * * * It was close work for James
to part from his mother, and it was no less so for me to
part from my dear and faithful companion, but committing
him to the keeping of Israel's unslumbering Shepherd, I
bade him affectionately farewell, with very little if any
expectation of ever meeting again upon earth ; but with
the trembling yet cheering hope of rejoining my dear
friend where partings are no more.

" First day, 25th.— * * * Just before the ship was
under sail, our friends Thomas and Matilda Simey came
off in a boat with three of their children, and brought us
a goat to give us a little milk for our tea, which was a
great addition to our comfort, there being nothing of the
kind on board.

BREAKWATER AND

"First day, 1st mo. 20th, 1856— * * * On reaching Gravesend we cast anchor until the turn of the tide, when I availed myself of the opportunity of going on shore with the pilot, and finding a train just starting for London, took my place and came up to the city. * * * Wrote a few lines soon after I got in to inform my dear wife of my arrival, and to say that I hoped to be with them on third day, if the Lord permit. Thus through the mercy and goodness of my Heavenly Father have I been permitted, after an absence of three years and a half to a day, once more to set my feet upon the shores of my native land.

LAST JOURNEY.

AFTER spending about a year and a half at home, my father felt it his duty to set out again on a visit of Gospel love to distant lands. My mother accompanied him on this last journey, and was a great comfort and help to him. They spent upwards of two years in visiting the United States (including Iowa, Minnesota, and Kansas, then only newly settled, and where they had to put up with many privations and rough accommodation), Canada, and Nova Scotia. They then set out for California, and went by sea, crossing the Isthmus of Panama by rail, there being no railway across the continent at that time. My mother's journal, written for her children, gives an account of their subsequent travels.

" 20th 6th mo., 1859, New York.—Went on board the ' Star of the West,' bound to Panama, and were glad to find that, owing to some opposition, instead of a thousand passengers, who have sometimes gone out in this steamer, we have under four hundred.

" 25th.—We have had rough and squally weather for the most part since coming on board, and the rain has sometimes fallen in torrents. General sickness has prevailed, from the strong man to women and children. Oh! this soul-sickening, heart-loathing feeling! how it prostrates both body and mind!

" 27th, at Havanna, Island of Cuba.—On rising this

morning we heard joyous voices, and found ourselves approaching the city. * * Having obtained leave to proceed, we were soon alongside the coal wharf, which is on the opposite side of the bay to the city, where the boat remained until five o'clock in the evening. In the meantime the passengers amused themselves in various ways. Some hired small boats, and were rowed across the bay to the city, where they had to pay a dollar for a permit. For another dollar they were driven through the city and round the suburbs in a carriage with long shafts and large heavy wheels, drawn by a mule, on which the driver rides. On returning, they reported that the streets of the city were not more than eighteen or twenty feet wide, with narrow footpaths, on which there was only just room for one person to pass another. Awnings are stretched across the streets, which are paved with stone, and have a gutter down the middle. The city and suburbs extend over several miles, but look more inviting at a distance than upon closer inspection. The houses are slight frame buildings, some white, and others variously coloured blue, pink, red or green.

"7th mo. 2nd.—After a voyage of twelve days we arrived at Aspinwall, on the Isthmus of Panama, about two p.m. The sky was overcast, and the rain falling. A few hotels, stores, and native huts were all that I saw of this city. We had to walk a short distance to the railway depôt, and were soon surrounded by coloured persons offering cakes and fruit for sale. All was bustle and confusion for a short time. We had to hire a man to carry some of our many little things, which we had under our own care. The train was soon in motion. The country through which we passed abounded in tropical fruits. Palms, bananas, and several kinds of tall broad-leaved shrubs were growing in wild profusion. Some of the ferns were several yards high. For many miles the country was flat and very swampy, but as we proceeded it became more hilly and picturesque. The soil is red,

and the sides of the hills exhibit iron ore. In some
places workmen were engaged in getting stone out of the
hills. Gliding along, we passed several native villages
and little huts scattered along our track. They are of the
most simple construction, consisting of a high roof covered
with various sorts of leaves, and supported by sticks or
boards. Some of the huts were open at the front. The
inmates hailed our approach with seeming pleasure.
Some of the women and girls were partly dressed in
white; others had but little covering, and many of the
children were naked. * * * Before reaching the city of
Panama the shades of darkness gathered around us, so
that we had only an indistinct view of the place, but it
appeared much larger than Aspinwall, and the buildings
more substantial. On arriving at the railway terminus a
general bustle took place, and we were soon crowded into
a small steamboat, which took us to the large and elegant
steamer the 'Golden Age,' where we found ourselves surrounded by increasing comforts, having one of the best
rooms, containing a bed, sofa, and ample room to turn
ourselves.

" Second day, 4th.—Yesterday was one of unsettle-
ment. All the luggage was taken on board the previous
night; but we sailed soon after daylight. On leaving the
Bay of Panama we found the ocean studded with small
islands of a conical form, which looked verdant and beautiful at this season of the year. We passed several
isolated rocks. The Pacific was smooth, and scarcely a
wave ruffled its surface.

" Sixth day, 8th.—Found ourselves only six miles
from Acapulco, a Mexican port, where we expect to stay
some hours to take in coal, water, &c. The town only
looks like a scattered country village. Some tamarind
trees were pointed out to us, which looked like wide-
spreading apple trees. Numerous boats were soon alongside of us, some to convey passengers who wished to

visit the town ; other boats contained native fruits, coral,
and shells for sale ; but as the natives are not allowed to
come on board, they have an ingenious plan of trading.
When our passengers wished to purchase anything, after
making a bargain as to the price, a green orange was
tied to the end of a cord by the trader, which he threw
on board our vessel, and to the other end of the cord he
tied a satchel containing the articles agreed for, which
being drawn up and secured, the money was returned in
the satchel. We were much amused with watching the
movements of about half a dozen natives who were swimming around us for three hours. Some of the passengers
threw silver coin into the water, when two of the compe-
titors would immediately dive, and in a short time rise
again ; the one bearing the prize shewing it in his hand,
and then depositing it in his mouth. They displayed
wonderful agility in the art of swimming. Some of them
were copper-coloured, with black curling hair. The Bay
of Acapulco is rather small, but nicely sheltered by rocky
ranges of mountains. Palm and other fruit trees grow
around the native huts upon the plain. In the evening
we enjoyed sitting upon the lower deck watching the
lightning burst from the clouds, by which many of the
mountains are capped. Thermometer 88° in our room
to-day.

" Seventh day, 16th, San Francisco, California.—About
half-past six last evening we came in sight of the Tele-
graph Station, situate upon a high hill, eight miles from
the city. On a near approach we observed two or three
barren-looking hills scattered over with buildings even to
their summits. The Bay is very commodious, but open
and much exposed to the winds. On reaching the wharf,
we were almost alarmed at seeing the crowd of persons
who were awaiting the arrival of the steamer, and our
saloons were soon filled by persons apparently looking for
old acquaintances or relations. All was noise, bustle, and
confusion, whilst we stood unclaimed upon the deck, until

a respectable-looking man, who had been apprised of our coming, made his appearance; when, after forcing our way through the crowd, in danger of falling into the water, he conducted us to a coach, and went with us to the Oriental Hotel, where he and his family were boarding. * * San Francisco is a most singular looking place; its extent being about three miles by three and a half. Its population is seventy thousand. It is a succession of hills and valleys. Sometimes in going up the hills we are up to the ancles in sand, and then come abruptly upon a solid surface, like hard rock; but it is only the hard earth, upon which even the heavy rain seems to have little effect. From the middle of the fifth month to the latter end of the tenth is the dry season, wherein they rarely have a shower of rain. The dews are sometimes pretty heavy; but the country has a parched and dry appearance.

"Alameda, San José Valley, 27th.—The accounts we hear of the unusual fruitfulness of California would be deemed fabulous, if they were not well authenticated. Two hundred bushels of potatoes have been produced from one acre, some weighing six pounds each. Onions so large as to cover a dessert plate, water melons weighing sixty pounds, and pumpkins two hundred pounds each. In the early settlement of the State fruits and vegetables were very scarce. Six years ago a small peach cost three dollars, and apples were three dollars each. An individual raised a crop of potatoes which sold for one hundred and eighty thousand dollars. Owing to the high price, such an abundance were grown the following year, that the market was overstocked, and some of the potatoes rotted in the ground; consequently, the man whose gains had been so abundant, lost great part of them again.

"San Francisco, 5th of 8th mo.—Some of our kind friends in Philadelphia and New York have furnished us with about fifteen hundred volumes of books for distribution in California, besides which some have been sent

from London, and others have been purchased by ourselves
from a fund kindly placed in our hands by our friends at
home, and they occupy considerable time in sorting and
distributing.   Called upon a family this morning who are
members of our Society, and have been resident here six
years; but were not previously aware that there were a
number of others in the city like-minded with themselves.
They are not in the habit of attending any place of
worship. * * * Our arrival in this State having been
announced in the newspapers, and also by private letters,
we do not seem to require much introduction. * * *

   "First day, 11th.—Drove three miles through an
avenue of willows, planted in former times by the
Spaniards, to San José, a little busy, improving city,
where the Jesuits formed a church.   There is a large
female seminary belonging to the Catholics, and a large
Catholic Church.   Many of the old Spanish houses are
still standing; they are one storey high, with heavy
overhanging roofs.   Having the address of some persons
here, we obtained further information at an hotel in the
city, and rode to the house of Asa Vestal, where we were
kindly greeted, and requested to alight. * * * It was
quite a treat to look at A. V.'s grape vines, which are
about the size of nut bushes, and so loaded with grapes
that the branches need supporting.   It is susposed that
the vineyard will produce 20,000lb weight of fruit this
year, the wholesale price of which is threepence per lb.
Water and other melons cover a considerable space of
ground.   A pumpkin was grown in this garden which
weighed 264lbs.   There were others which we saw
growing that were as thick as a man's body.   The soil
is like the finest powder, and appears dry upon the
surface, but when moved it is found to be damp within
three inches of the top.   Vines, melons, and various
vegetables require no watering at this season of the year;
but the flowers require frequent artificial moisture.   A
small animal called the gopher, of the mole kind, is very

destructive, sometimes knawing the fruit-trees off by the
roots. Squirrels are also abundant, and very troublesome.

"Angel's Camp. * * * —Being in the vicinity of the
Big Trees, we made half a day's journey to see them.
For the last fourteen miles the road lay through a
mountain forest, where we noticed many fine trees.
Only two mean dwelling houses lay in our track. On
the slope of the Sierra Nevada Mountains, in Calaveras
County, we first got sight of the little clearing on which
the Big Tree Hotel presents a welcome sight to the
tourist. Two noble trees stand as sentinels on each
side the road at the entrance. There is a grove extend-
ing over a quarter of a mile, where about ninety of the
largest trees were first discovered in 1853. The first
which caught our eye was the trunk of one which had
been cut down to within six feet of the ground, the top
of which my husband measured, and found it to be
twenty-five feet in diameter, exclusive of the bark. It
was enclosed, and made a very large circular summer
house, the top of the stump forming the floor, which was
very close grained and sound. Near it lay a part of the
same tree lengthwise, against which a ladder was placed,
and by ascending twenty-six steps, the summit of its side
was gained. The largest tree in the grove, called the
Father of the Forest, has fallen down, and lays in a state
of decay. Its diameter at the bottom is twenty-nine feet,
and from its remains it is supposed to have been four
hundred feet high. A ladder is placed against it to
enable persons to walk upon it. The Mother of the
Forest is surrounded by scaffolding, which was erected
some years ago, for the purpose of stripping off the bark
about half way up, portions of which have been sent to
various parts of the world. At three feet from the ground
this tree is seventy-seven feet in circumference. The
bark is from one foot to fifteen inches thick, and its
computed height three hundred and thirty-seven feet.

It seems perfectly sound, but bears the marks of much violence by individuals chopping and cutting pieces from it. The wood is red like cedar. Another tree, named Hercules, at three feet from the ground, is thirty feet in circumference. Of the eight trees which my husband measured, the smallest was fifty-three feet in circumference, and Hercules is supposed to be three hundred and twenty feet high. From calculations made from the rings, these trees are said to be from three hundred to four hundred years old. They are as straight as an arrow, and the foliage, which is something between the pine and the arbor vitæ, commences about half way from the top. They have small cones, while the sugar pines, which grow in the same grove, have cones half a yard long, which look very graceful as they hang from the tips of the lofty branches. Some of the giant trees grow in pairs, about three feet apart, and three, named the Graces, stand alongside each other in majestic grandeur. I have mentioned the bark as being more than one foot thick; but it is light, and has the appearance of turf.

" First day, 9th, 10th mo., at Grass Valley.—The persons whose names had been given us as residing in Neveda having removed, we came to this place yesterday. On alighting from the stage a man accosted my husband, calling him by name, saying his name was Delano, and that his wife had come along with us from New York to San Francisco, and would be glad to see us. On making enquiry, it seemed needful to write to some persons at a distance to meet us here, where arrangements were made for a public meeting to be held this evening. In the afternoon we paid a visit to Alonzo and Mary Delano. Alonzo has been in California about two years, during which time he has had many reverses of fortune. He gave us some interesting particulars respecting the native Indians. In 1850 he was the only white man residing amongst the Indians fifty miles north of this place, and kept a general store, which they were in the habit of frequenting. Having endeavoured to gain their confidence by just dealing, he succeeded in doing so, and they lived together peaceably, and he could leave his store under their charge. Having occasion to go to Marysville, he informed them of it, and said he expected to be away six sleeps, and he should leave his beef, cloth, and other stores under their care, and they must take charge of the tent, and let no person enter. Accordingly he departed; but was detained longer than he expected on account of sickness; and finding it needful to go to Sacramento he became uneasy, thinking the Indians would consider him unfaithful to his promise. After being absent thirteen days, he reached a river, on the opposite side of which his tent was pitched. An Indian observing him got a log and took him across; and although he saw other Indians standing round, no one seemed to welcome him as usual, it having formerly been their practice to surround him, when one would take charge of his horse, a second would bring wood, and a third water, &c. On entering his store, the door of which was made up with brushwood, as a sign that no one must enter, he was dismayed to find that everything had been removed; but he made no complaint. Looking round, he noticed an aged Indian approaching him, who, looking stedfastly upon him, said, ' You go away, and say you stay six sleeps.' Then producing a cord upon which six knots had been tied, he continued, ' But you stay away thirteen sleeps;' counting seven more knots. Delano looking him in the face, replied, ' I was sick two sleeps, I was two sleeps in going to Sacramento, and three sleeps in returning.' Then the Indian said ' Good!' and became open and friendly with him, which the other Indians observing, came round him at once, and he was informed that some bad Americans were going to rob his tent, so his goods had been removed. He then enquired for the Chief, and having been conducted to him, found him sitting on a skin which was spread upon the ground. Being invited to sit down beside the Chief, after an interval of silence, Alonzo was charged with not having fulfilled his engagement, when a similar explanation took place as before; at the conclusion of which the Chief assented that the reasons were good. Alonzo then said, ' I left my stores under the care of the Indians ;' which being assented to, the Chief pointed to his wigwam, and said they had been removed there ; and calling to some Indians, about a dozen came, and in half an hour the goods were replaced in Alonzo's store, not even the hammer and nails being wanting.

" San Francisco, seventh day.—Walked out this morning. We went to see the Chinese Temple. Entering a door from the street, we proceeded along two narrow passages, out of which several doors opened into filthy-looking dwellings. We then found ourselves in a narrow yard, on one side of which stood the temple. The exterior had various Chinese inscriptions upon it. In the basement storey arm chairs were set, and numerous little tables. Several Chinese were going to and fro ; but they seemed to take little notice of us. On making signs to one of them that we wished to inspect the place, he pointed to a narrow dirty staircase, on ascending which and going along a passage we entered a room, which seemed to be their most holy place. Over the altar hung two brazen shields, in which some little images like dolls, dressed in Chinese costume, were placed. In a recess beyond, gaudy-looking pictures and other et ceteras were exhibited. A lamp was suspended, wherein incense was burning, as well as a smaller light. We met two men coming out of the room, but we were left alone ; and as there was no one to give us information, we came away quite disappointed to find the temple such a dirty and mean-looking place.

" Second day, 31st.— * * * During our stay at Placerville I became a little acquainted with a Mexican woman who was a guest at the hotel. She spoke French and Spanish, and just enough English to enable us to

converse. She inquired if I was a Catholic, and on my
saying that I was a Protestant, she replied that she was
also. Her first husband was a Frenchman, who dying,
she married an American, who seems very kind and
attentive to her, and is taking great pains to teach her
the English language. The Mexicans are dark com-
plexioned, with black hair, thick eyebrows, and there is
a deep expression in their somewhat downcast black eyes.
They have the character of being naturally cruel and
treacherous. On asking for our bill this morning, our
noble-hearted host replied that he kept all ministers free
of charge—a favour that we rarely meet with. Took the
stage at nine a.m., and came fifteen miles to Georgetown,
partly on a road cut out of the sides of the mountain
ranges, and very steep, so that on going up hill the
horses could only just keep the carriage moving. At
the bottom of one ravine we crossed the south fork of
the American River, which is nearly dry at present.
Some Chinese had confined the water to a narrow stream,
and were engaged in cradling—a process which I have
not seen before—mining in California being now generally
done in a more wholesale way. We passed through several little mining towns. In the course of our journey
we saw several Indians. One woman had her child tied
to a board, which she carried in her arms. A man,
accompanied by his squaw, carried his bow and arrows,
and a third squaw, whose only covering seemed to be an
old skirt hung round her neck, with one arm and shoulder
exposed, carried a basket upon her back. Reached
Georgetown to a late dinner, and as your dear father
felt a drawing to have a public meeting in the evening,
notices had to be written and posted. This town was
burned down some time since, and several brick buildings
are in course of erection. There being no meeting houses,
the theatre seemed the most convenient building to meet
in, and, considering the short notice, there was a good
attendance, and I trust the Lord opened the hearts of
many to receive the things which were spoken.

" Salem, Oregon, sixth day, 9th 12th mo.— * * *
We find the Supreme Court of the State is in session,
and the Governor, chief justice, and other officers are
staying at the same hotel as ourselves, which, though
only a second-rate place, is the best in the town, which
is the capital of Oregon. In this levelling country all
stand upon equal ground; professors and profane, the
Governor and officers, sit down indiscriminately at the
same table as the mechanic and stable boy, and all are
attended upon alike. Such mixtures were very unpleasant
to me when first setting out upon our travels, and I dislike them still, though they must be borne. Sometimes
young men who are entire strangers will undertake to
question us, and compare our little Island with their
large Continent and its many resources. A youngster
of this class told us a few days ago that Oregon was
about as far advanced as England was twenty-five years
ago. We could only smile at his arrogance. Father
has obtained leave to have the use of the Court-house
for a public meeting to-morrow evening, and has employed
a man to sweep out the upper room and stairs—an operation but seldom performed.

" Eleventh, 12th mo.—To-morrow we expect to go
eight or ten miles into the country to visit some families,
and on leaving here we have to stop at several places on
going down the Willamette before we reach Portland, our
place of embarkation for the north. The circumstance
of our being here at the time when the Supreme Court is
sitting has given opportunity of placing books illustrative
of our peaceable principles in the hands of those who are
in authority. * * * Sat down together to wait upon the
Lord this morning for a renewal of our spiritual strength,
and our waiting was not in vain : our minds were solem-
nized and, I trust, strengthened in the faithfulness of our
merciful High Priest and Intercessor with the Father,
who was not unmindful of His unworthy children. We
have had calls from various individuals.

L

" Second day, 12th.—Hired a light waggon this morning, and drove eight miles to the house of Samuel Simmons, passing through a fine district of enclosed prairie land and one forest of fine timber. Found our friends living on what is called Howell's Prairie, where they settled about fourteen years ago amongst the Indians and wolves, and endured many privations. The farm, consisting of six hundred and forty acres, is now divided, and their children are settled upon it. During the last four or five years the farmers have had a great source of wealth from the growth of apples. S. S. has some large orchards, which have been remarkably productive. Last year the wholesale price was from twelve to twenty cents per pound; but much attention having been paid to this profitable mode of money-making, the markets have been well supplied this year, and the price has fallen to from four to seven cents per pound. When ripe they are carefully packed in wooden boxes holding from forty to fifty pounds weight, and shipped to California, &c. * * *

" Third day, 13th.—After dressing this morning father was shown to the pump to wash himself, and had to walk over the icy ground on his way to it. I was privileged to have some water brought into the kitchen in a tin dish. Although considered wealthy, this family have no female servant, but the weakly mother and the son's wife, who has a young child, have to do the work of the house. * * *

" Victoria, Vancouver's Island, 9th 1st mo., 1860.— Since coming here we have had frosty nights and showery days. Four or five weeks ago there was a fall of snow about two feet deep, and some still lays upon the surrounding hills, but the settlers seem to think the winter is nearly over. The wages for hired servants seem to be as high here as they are in California and Oregon. The keeper of this hotel informed us that he paid seventy-five dollars a month for his cook, and other men servants

want two-and-a-half to three dollars per day besides
their board. The French are excellent cooks, and we had
also the privilege of a cleanly spread table with bright
knives and spoons, a luxury we seldom find in these re-
mote districts. To-morrow we are expecting to proceed
northward in the direction of Frazer's River to visit one
or more new settlements. * * *

"Victoria, seventh day, 21st.—Yesterday was one of
suspense, but in the evening we were notified that the
steamboat would not leave until noon to-day. Father
having felt concerned respecting the neglected condition
of the Indians in these parts, of whom there are from
one thousand to fifteen hundred around Victoria, had an
interview with Bishop Hills on the subject this morning,
and it is interesting to find that his attention is turned
to the subject, and it appears that something is about to
be done for their moral and religious instruction. Going
on board the steamboat we were accosted by an intelligent
Indian who could speak a little English. He produced a
certificate with which he had been furnished by an officer
on board one of the ships of war, in which he is described
as Lord Jim, Chief of one of the tribes, and of good
character, &c. Leaving the Bay of Victoria we entered
Puget Sound, intending to cross over to Port Townsend,
a distance of thirty-five miles. After being out from one
to two hours the sea became rough, and I thought it best
to lie down. The billows rose higher and higher, the
earthenware began to upset, and the furniture in the
cabin to be displaced. The wind being directly ahead,
and our frail bark not being able to make way against it,
the captain considered it safest to retire into the harbour,
which we reached at three p.m. Two hours later the
wind increased to a gale, and although close to the wharf
our boat seemed ready to be torn from her moorings. In
a few hours the wind died away, the tempest was hushed,
and a calm succeeded.

" First day, 22nd.—About half-past seven a.m. our boat was again upon its way. After breakfast we retired to our state room and read the 107th Psalm. In the succeeding silence our hearts were deeply prostrated before the Lord, under a renewed feeling of His merciful care and protection over the unworthy workmanship of His holy hand. The weather cloudy but mild and calm. Took exercise upon deck, and had a partial view of the distant mountains, some of which are covered with snow all the year round. Passed Smith's and Whidby's Islands and the harbour of Dungenness. Arrived at Port Townsend before noon, where we left mail bags, and stayed an hour. We thought there were as many Indians as white men standing on the wharf. Some of the former were well dressed, and their faces were besmeared with red paint. A number of squaws and children were squatted upon the ground. Their huts are covered with matting, and extend along the shore. Continuing our voyage southward down Puget Sound, we stopped a short time at Port Ludlow, a small settlement of about twenty houses, with Indian huts around. Our next calling place was Port Gambill, where the Indians came to us in their small canoes, and I observed a considerable Indian village on the opposite side of the bay. These, and several other places which we shall pass in the night, are supported by the lumbering business. The Indian tribes around Puget Sound have had reservations assigned, but many still remain around the settlements of the whites. It is pleasant to hear that agents are appointed, and some pains are taken to instruct the children, and to teach the young men handicraft trades.

" Victoria, 2nd 2nd mo.— * * * This morning we called upon the Governor, James Douglas, who is an estimable man, and of noble stature and bearing. In speaking of the Indians, he expressed his desire for their moral and religious improvement as soon as measures could be taken and carried into execution. At the

present time they are suffering from the introduction of
the vices of the white man, which is truly a mournful
consideration. The governor's wife is of Indian descent,
and does not appear to mingle much in general society.
One of his daughters sat with us, and in course of conversation remarked to me how difficult they found it to
get women servants; so much so that they found it
needful to do their work themselves, sensibly saying that
such being the case it was best to do it cheerfully. The
Indians are employed in cutting wood and other menial
things, but in general they do not like constant employment. We have visited one school here where the Indian,
African, and white children are upon a level; but, painful
to say, there exists almost as much prejudice in the
Americans against the poor Indians as against the
negroes, and some would clear them from the face of
the earth if not restrained by law. It has many times
been cause of humble thankfulness to ourselves that such
an open door has been set before us as regards holding
public meetings since coming on this side the American
continent, and it is rather singular that the first obstruction
we have met with is in this colony. In a former letter I
mentioned our meeting with Dr. Hills, the newly-appointed
Bishop of British Columbia, upon whom father has called
a few times since our arrival in Victoria. Having a prospect of appointing a meeting at Esquimault, a small
place three miles from Victoria, on looking round our
friends thought there was no place so likely as a building
recently put up there by general subscription, and which
is occupied by the Episcopal minister, one of Bishop
Hill's clergy, which they seemed to think there would
be no objection to our having the use of; but on mentioning the subject to the minister and the bishop they
gave a decided refusal, with the remark that if they
opened it to us they might even have an application
from the Mormons for the same purpose; and on understanding that we wished to invite the inhabitants to
the meeting, the reply was that *they* could take care of

them. The minister, Dundas, took offence from seeing an advertisement of a meeting to be held in Victoria by Robert Lindsey and wife, ministers of the Society of Friends from England, to which the public were respectfully invited, expressing his surprise at our assuming the name of ministers, as he considered the Church of England was the only true Church, and they being the successors of the Apostles, had the exclusive right to ordain ministers.

" San Francisco, second day, 13th.—We left Victoria on fourth day evening, and for two days and three nights had very rough weather, and much sickness prevailed, in which we had our share. I kept my berth almost entirely for two days. * * * About half-past five p.m. we were safely landed in this city, and once more took up our quarters at the International Hotel. The distance from Victoria to this place is nine hundred miles. Since leaving here, near three months ago, we have travelled about three thousand miles ; and having been enabled to perform the service which seemed to be required, and been brought back in safety and in peace, our hearts are prostrated before the Lord under a feeling of His goodness and mercy in leading about and instructing His unworthy children, and keeping them as the apple of the eye, to whom, with our merciful High Priest and Intercessor with the Father, who is touched with a feeling of our infirmities, be glory for ever and ever. Amen. * * * I have before spoken of the Indians around Victoria, and of their broad countenances, and have since been told that the head is compressed and flattened in childhood, which appears to be the cause. I noticed some Indians who wore what looked like a small silver button between the lower lip and the chin for the purpose of drawing out the under lip, which, to our view, only adds to their deformity.

" San Francisco, 17th 3rd mo.—This morning we had

a long walk to the Lone Mountain Cemetery, where the
citizens have one hundred and sixty acres appropriated
for a burying ground. The site is well chosen, com-
manding a view of both the city and ocean. Some costly
monuments are erected, which, I think, is money ill spent.
I much prefer a simple stone, surrounded by green grass
and overhanging trees. We were taken into a vault
where the bodies of Chinamen are deposited. They are
made up in lead coffins, which are placed in strong wooden
cases, and placed upon the ground, &c., ready to be transported into China. The bodies of the lower classes are
buried in a piece of ground appropriated for the purpose,
and when decomposed the bones are carefully gathered,
washed, and spread out to dry, and then put into separate
boxes ready for shipment to China. I do not know
whether they think women have souls, but they are not
worth transportation. On our return we had to wait
some time at a country hotel for an omnibus; so we
walked into a beautiful garden, where we saw apple and
pear trees in blossom, and peas in pod. In the afternoon
a Japanese ambassador and others, with about fifty at-
tendants, arrived here from Jeddo on their way to
Washington, five of whom were at our hotel. They
are attired in a loose blue dress, something like the
Chinese, whom they resemble in person, but are darker
in complexion.

" First day, 18th.—This morning we had an appointed
meeting in a large public room, to which the citizens were
invited. Some hundreds were present, and were very
solid and well-behaved. It was a good meeting, and
mercifully owned by Him who remains to be the crown
and diadem of all rightly gathered assemblies. Father
was enabled to preach the Gospel, desiring all might
believe and obey its doctrines and precepts. Those in
authority were exhorted to be faithful to their trust, not
as men pleasers, but as those who must give an account.
They were reminded that ' righteousness exalteth a nation,

but sin is a reproach to any people.' A warning was given against a continuance in sin, lest the Lord's judgments should come upon them, as was the case with his chosen people formerly. Much more of a searching and awakening nature was communicated, and prayers arose for the Lord's blessing upon the bread which had been broken amongst us. The 'Francis Palmer,' by which we expect to sail to Honolulu, arrived here from that port yesterday, and is expected to return the latter end of this week. The prospect of a release from this part of the Lord's vineyard is pleasant; though in looking forward we feel sensible that many hardships and dangers still await us; but having been mercifully helped hitherto, and cared for beyond what we could ask or think, it would be ungrateful to call in question the faithfulness of our God. * * *

" 22nd 3rd mo. 1860.—This evening we had a farewell meeting with a few choice Friends on whose behalf we felt much interested, and were strengthened to be faithful to apprehended duty in expressing what arose in our hearts. At the close of the meeting we were presented with a certificate addressed to our Monthly, Quarterly, and Yearly Meetings, expressing the unity our Friends had felt with our company and services. Having now accomplished the work which father felt called for at his hands in these parts, we are favoured with peace of mind. We have received orders to go on board the 'Francis Palmer' in the morning.

" 11th 4th mo.—On looking out this morning were glad to find ourselves alongside the Island of Molokai, the east end of which presents high perpendicular cliffs, and the west sloping high land. The Island of Oahu was soon visible; its length is about forty miles and its breadth fifteen miles. It is mountainous with sharp peaks; the most prominent of which is an extinct volcano. The hills have a barren aspect, but the intermediate valleys seem green. After heading Diamond Point we entered the spacious Bay of Honolulu, when a pilot came on board, and we were drawn to shore by a steam tug. The native huts extend along the shore for some miles amidst rows of cocoa nut trees. Reefs of coral form a lengthy bar; but there is a natural passage through marked by buoys. The town of Honolulu has a rural appearance stretched along the beach, and the suburbs running up a valley encircled by mountains, upon which the clouds often rest, and frequently water the surrounding neighbourhood. I remained on board feeling like a stranger in a distant land, whilst father went to the Custom House, where he paid one dollar for a permit to land our luggage, and a tax of four dollars for the benefit of the hospital. A number of the town's people soon came to hear the news, &c., to several of whom I was introduced. Amongst the rest was Prince Lot, a large, stout, well-dressed man, who is the King's brother. There being no respectable hotels in the town, lodgings had been engaged for us at William Humphreys, (who, with his wife, formerly lived at Brighton), to whose house we were taken up a shady lane, and after alighting at a garden gate, were met by our hostess, and shown into a room on the ground floor, with an outer door shaded by trees, which had been appropriated to our use, and being of a good size, serves for both bed and sitting room. We were glad to find the terms moderate, fifteen dollars a-week for board and lodging for both of us.

"Honolulu, Oahu, 13th, sixth day.— * * * On walking towards the foot of the mountains, we passed some native market gardens where we noticed banana and other trees laden with fruit. The common food of the natives is a root called taro, which is grown in swampy ground, and cooked in various ways. When simply boiled and sliced, it has the appearance of bread; but the natives mash and make it into what is called poi, which is put into calabashes, and carried about for sale. The poi-makers have a pole with a small white flag attached

flying from their dwellings, some of which are covered
with matting or hay, and others are good frame houses.
We do not find the weather quite so oppressive as we
expected, and are informed that the thermometer does
not often rise higher than 86° in summer, nor sink below
50° in winter.

" 14th, seventh day.—Called upon one of the oldest
missionaries, Ephraim Weston Clark, who, along with
his wife, we had previously seen in San Francisco.   He
was here when our valued friend Daniel Wheeler visited
the Islands, and seems to be a worthy, pious man.   He
preaches in a large stone church which was erected by
the natives twenty years since.   Its dimensions are one
hundred and forty by eighty feet.   From one thousand
to fifteen hundred natives attend this place of worship.
where they hear the Gospel in their own language,
E. W. Clark has a large and interesting family.   On
returning we went round by the shore, but found it
very flat, and there were so many pools of water that we
were prevented from walking with any degree of comfort.
We passed some native huts, and had an opportunity of
seeing one family take their mid-day meal out of a hollow
place in the ground where it had been cooked.   It consisted of a small pig enclosed in ti-tree leaves, tied up at
each end.   Another bundle was said to contain the liver,
&c., and potatoes were laid round the sides.   Heated
stones are put under and over the victuals, and the whole
is then covered with leaves.   The process of cooking
occupies from three to four hours.   The man who was
superintending could speak English, and he informed us
that the dinner was for some men whom we saw loading
a boat with coral.   We have also seen the native operation
of washing clothes.   They are carried to a rivulet (across
which a dam is made for the occasion) and laid upon a
board or stone, where, after being wet and rubbed with
soap, they are kneaded, and beaten with a piece of wood
something like a rolling-pin, while fresh water is supplied

by the hand from the brook. We did not see the finishing process. From four o'clock on seventh day afternoon is a time of general recreation for the natives, and we see young men and women riding at full gallop; but our feelings were shocked to see the women mounted in the attitude of men; but by means of a long printed scarf tied round the waist, the ends of which reach below the feet, and are confined and thrust through the stirrups, their limbs are covered. Most of the women have a very dignified, bold, and masculine appearance. They are very erect, and generally tall and stout. Some of their countenances are lively and interesting. At these times they appear to be dressed in their best clothes, and many of them have a very novel appearance. Their outside covering is a dress made in the form of a loose night-gown, the material varying from white or printed cotton and stuffs of various hue, to yellow, purple, and other colours of silk and flowered satin. Most of the young women are decked with garlands of roses or other gay flowers or green boughs. Unlike most of the aborigines of other places, they do not seem to have been trained to habits of industry, but spend much of their time in sitting upon the ground, and lounging about the streets and houses; and their dislike to exertion is so great that they have been known to go without food for a day rather than dig up and prepare the taro for a meal. Five years since the smallpox raged on these Islands, by which some thousands of the natives died, and they continue to decrease in number.

" Honolulu, fourth day, 25th.—The Supreme Court has been sitting upwards of two weeks; but it is now over, and the members are more at liberty. It is concluded to hold a meeting with the natives on first day morning, and another for the public on second day evening. Spent the afternoon at Thomas Brown's. Business detained him in town until near sunset, but we much enjoyed the company of his wife. Called upon Captain Paty's

wife, and felt it a privilege to inhale the fresh air of the
Nuuarm Valley. We passed a rude hut near which two
men were seated upon the ground preparing taro. The
roots had been placed upon a long, shallow, wooden dish,
and having been beaten with a wooden instrument something like a potato-crusher, had the appearance of dough.
A calabash containing water was placed beside them, out
of which they took the fluid, using their hands as a ladle.
The process of poi-making is very laborious, but families
often make enough at one time to last a week, as it is all
the better for being a little acid. When eating, fingers
supply the place of knife, fork, or spoon.

" 30th, second day.—There are about seven thousand
natives and two thousand foreigners on this island. Honolulu is the only town, but the inhabitants are scattered
over the valleys. The soil of the Sandwich Islands is
formed of decomposed volcanic rocks, sand, mud, and
ashes. To be made fruitful it requires constant irriga-
tion. During the last ten days the thermometer has
stood at about 70° in the morning, and has risen to 84°
at noon several times. We have just been to look at
a vessel bearing the name of 'Emma Rooke,' which is
expected to sail for the Island of Maui to-morrow afternoon, by which we intend to proceed to Lahaina, which
is the chief town.

" Lahaina, Island of Maui, 7th day 5th of 5th month.—
After a very suffering voyage of forty-eight hours, during
which we had frequent detentions from calms and head
winds, we anchored outside the reefs at four p.m. yesterday, and were rowed ashore in a small boat, our fellow-
passenger rendering us efficient help. During the passage
we had ample opportunity of observing the customs of the
natives, who spread mats, bundles, or pillows on the deck,
and reclined or sat upon them. Each party had calabashes,
some of which contained poi, fish, and seaweed. Three
times a day the stores were opened, and one set of fingers

after another was dipped into the pasty substance, and
conveyed to the mouth. The dried or salted fish was
torn asunder by the fingers or the teeth, the dried
seaweed forming a relish. I saw one young woman
pare a raw sweet potato with her teeth, and afterwards
bite from one end. The meal being ended, all is again
covered up, and a calabash containing water passed round,
in which they wash their hands. Some of the women
put up shades, and others use umbrellas to screen themselves from the sun. At night they lie down side by side
with their dogs, covering themselves with a blanket.
They are very fond of going from one island to another,
and when inclination prompts, if they have only a single
dollar, they will pay it for their passage. We had letters
of introduction to parties here, and through the kindness
of one of them we have met with very airy and comfortable
quarters in a one-storey grass house, erected many years
ago at an elevation of only three feet above the shore,
and within fifteen yards of the Pacific Ocean, for the
accommodation of Kamehameha III., the former king.
The native howe tree growing in front forms an agreeable
shade. Four small families take their meals in this house,
and one man is employed as cook and houseman. I have
not seen any fireplaces in the houses. The cooking is
done in outbuildings. Each of the families with whom
we are associated occupy separate cottages near each
other, where they live and sleep, but all meet at meal
times.

" Second day.— * * * Understanding there is a
settlement of foreigners in an agricultural district over
the mountains, father felt his mind drawn to visit them;
and as there is no carriage road, and I do not feel equal
to a journey of thirty-five miles on horseback, he set out
this morning accompanied by two natives as guides, expecting to return the latter end of the week. I have
been to see C. Bishop and wife, who, in addition to their
own two children, one of whom is an infant, have lately

undertaken the charge of eleven little girls from four to eight years of age, some half-caste and others natives, with a prospect of training them to habits of industry, order, and cleanliness, and affording them an asylum from the temptations to which they are subjected. A young woman is engaged as school teacher, who is instructing them in the English language. The expense of each child is calculated to be one hundred dollars a year, a part of which is contributed by those parents who are able, and the rest is made up by private subscription. The children are entirely under the care of their instructors, to whose control their parents have resigned them. * * * The natives are very fond of swimming. After wading some distance from the shore, they recline or lean with arms upon a board, which they raise to meet the waves, mounting each succeeding one with great dexterity. On returning to land they cast themselves with their board upon a large wave, and they are carried head foremost through the surf to the shore. We often notice the women wading in the water gathering seaweed. Opposite our window, apparently about three miles, but in reality ten miles distant, we see the Island of Lanai. To the right lies Molokai, and to the left Kaholawe, all mountainous, but gently sloping to the ocean. Lahaina is situated at the foot of lofty and broken mountains, in some of which are deep ravines. The town is much smaller than Honolulu. On this side the hills seem barren and void of timber, but I understand the other side is well covered with valuable trees. Sugar cane, grapes, and sweet potatoes are raised to advantage in some localities; cocoanut trees grow round many of the houses, and there are tamarind and bread-fruit trees. The castor oil shrub grows wild. The seed from which the oil is extracted is enclosed in a rough husk, and is said to contain a poisonous substance.

" 9th.—Last evening we took a walk to an extensive garden at the foot of the mountains, where we saw vines,

fig, vanana, bread-fruit, and cocoanut trees in full bearing.
I was presented with a piece of cocoanut cloth which
grows round the trunk of the trees, and protects the
young branches from injury.   But little rain falls in
Lahaina during the summer months, and however pleasant the idea of constant sunshine, it is very relaxing to
those who have been accustomed to a temperate climate.
We had frequent showers in Honolulu, and I am longing
for rain. Whilst writing I have to maintain a continuous
warfare with the mosquitoes, which keep alighting upon
my hands, &c.

" Lahaina, 11th.—Father arrived here from Makawao
about four p.m., much wearied in body, and reports that
the journey was one of the most difficult and dangerous
that he had ever travelled; but seems satisfied that it
has been accomplished. He had two meetings, one with
the foreigners and another with the natives, which appear
to have been satisfactory. The opposite side of the island
is described as being entirely different to this in climate,
soil, and produce. There are two sugar plantations belonging to foreigners on which native labourers are
employed. Wheat and oats are alike raised to profit.
There is a remarkable extinct volcano about twenty miles
from the missionary station at Makawao, which is said to
be nine thousand feet high, and the width across the crater
is ten miles; but father did not visit it.

" Honolulu, 17th.—This morning we attended a sitting
of the Missionaries' Yearly Meeting, when seventeen men,
with several of their wives and some children were present.
The first half-hour was devoted to religious exercises.
Many prayers were offered, and some counsel extended
previous to reading the reports, some of which were
lengthy and elaborate. It appears that there are eight
thousand children on these Islands who are educated in
the Hawaiian language, and only eight hundred who are
taught in the English language. The missionaries

have many difficulties to contend with, some of which might be avoided if their manner of worship was more simple. * * *

" Honolulu, 23rd.—On going to the wharf yesterday we found that the schooner was delayed sailing until this afternoon, so we took the opportunity of attending the opening of the Session of Legislature for these Islands, which sits once in two years.   The members of the Upper House, about twelve in number, were dressed in dark blue cloth embroidered with gold.   Twenty-six commissioners were present, two-thirds of whom were natives, and fine-looking men.   Many of the foreign residents attended as spectators.   The Japanese steamer arrived in this port on its return from California this morning, and the officers being invited on shore, had the opportunity of attending.   Twelve o'clock was the ap-pointed hour for the King to open the House in person. His approach was announced by the firing of cannon and martial music.   After the King's entrance the chaplain offered prayer in the Hawaiian tongue.   The King then read his speech, first in his native and then in the English language.   It contained especial mention of the necessity of increasing the number of training schools for young girls, whereby they might have their minds cultured, and be better prepared to become virtuous wives and mothers, and thus timely prevent the threatened extir-pation of their race.   On laying down the address the King immediately retired, and the assembly dispersed. On going outside we noticed a file of soldiers in attend-ance. The King entered a one-horse carriage, and without seeming to notice any one around him, took the reins, and drove off alone.   He is a tall, stout man, of bronze complexion, with good features.   He is unassuming in manner, and well educated, has good natural talents, and is said to be opposed to pomp and display.   With the exception of a star on his breast, the King's dress was that of a private gentleman.   The Governor of the Island of Oahu is the King's father, and is a fine, noble-looking man, apparently upwards of fifty years of age.

" Hilo, Island of Hawaii, 28th.—We arrived here yesterday afternoon after a voyage of four days. The distance from Honolulu to this place is two hundred and fifty miles, but the voyage is rendered irksome by the prevalence of head winds. We anchored off Lahaina, and went on shore for a few hours; but I felt so much exhausted as scarcely to be able to walk. Returned to the schooner in the evening, where we lay becalmed all night. Oh! the misery of sea-sickness! I can sometimes compare it to a feeling of exhaustion as between life and death, and the prostration which it induces in this tropical climate takes away all enjoyment of life. In these seasons I am too apt to give way to discouragement, thinking how far I am from home, and what large draughts of this kind of suffering I must yet endure ere I set my foot on the shores of dear old England. This Island is the largest in the group, being eighty-eight miles long and seventy-three broad. Hilo, the chief town, is situated in Byron's Bay, but is only the size of a small country village, and is said to contain not more than sixty white persons. Its chief trade is with the whale ships. There are about half a dozen merchants' stores in the place, including two or three kept by the Chinese. There has not been any late census taken of the natives; but the number upon the eight inhabited Islands is not supposed to be more than sixty thousand. Hilo is on the east side of the Island, from whence no high mountains are visible, but the land slopes gently to the water. We were landed here in a small boat, and there being no wharf, the natives carry the passengers on shore. We met with comfortable quarters at Captain J. Worth's, whose wife is a descendant of Friends, and seems much pleased to see us. We have a bed and sitting room over the Captain's store, in front of and within a few yards of the ocean. Much rain falls here,

M

and the Island has a very green appearance. Having
had a comfortable night's rest we are considerably revived, and enabled to take a little fresh courage, feeling
that the Lord hath not forsaken us, but is still mindful
of His unworthy children.

 " 31st.—A number of the white residents have been
to see us, and we have since called upon a missionary
and some other families, as well as visited two schools,
in one of which the English language is taught. We
found an interesting and intelligent class of young
people, to whom we gave books, &c., which were eagerly
received. We have also placed some books in the
hands of Dr. Whitmore as the commencement of a
public library.

 " Sixth mo. 1st.— * * * This evening I tried my
skill in horsemanship, and having a gentle little animal,
enjoyed a ride on the sea-shore. Father does not feel
his mind drawn to visit any of the other missionary
stations upon the Island, of which there are seven. The
wife of a missionary from the south coast has just arrived
here on a visit, having had a journey of seven days on
horseback. An opportunity offers, therefore, of sending
books to that distant field of labour. There are no carriages in Hilo; but some carts drawn by oxen, and one
or two little vehicles drawn by hand. There are good
roads in the village, but only trails beyond. Walked
one and a half miles to a sugar plantation worked by
Chinamen, and saw the process of sugar boiling. Some
of the canes are from two to three yards long, and about
the thickness of a man's wrist. It is crushed between
rollers worked by water power, then boiled to a certain
consistency, and put into frames to cool, from whence it
is taken to cylinders, and grained by means of a rapid
motion. Early this morning we felt a slight shock of an
earthquake.

"Hilo, third day.—Way not opening to leave this
Island until after next first day, and having some days
of leisure, we concluded to visit the noted active volcano
Kilauea, which is thirty-five miles from Hilo. Having
hired suitable horses, accompanied by John Worth and
three natives to carry our provisions, blankets, &c., we
took our departure at half-past seven a.m."

My mother's account of this journey being rather short
and imperfect, it is thought best to substitute that of a
visit paid by Hiram Bingham, an American missionary
to the Islands, extracted from a book written by him,
entitled, "A Residence of Twenty-one Years in the
Sandwich Islands." He says,—

"Approaching the great crater of Kilauea, we had
a fine view of the magnificent dome of Mauna Loa,
stretching on some twenty miles beyond it, and rising
above it to the lofty height of ten thousand feet. Evi-
dences of existing volcanic agency multiplied around us;
steam, gas, and smoke issued from sulphur banks on the
north-east and south-east sides of the crater, and here
and there from the deep and extended fissures connected
with the fiery subterranean agency; and as we passed
circumspectly along the apparently depressed plain that
surrounds the crater, we observed an immense volume of
smoke and vapour ascending from the midst of it. At
the same time, and from the same source, various unusual sounds, not easily described or explained, fell with
increasing intensity on the ear. Then the angry abyss,
the fabled habitation of Pele, the great ex-goddess of the
Hawaiians, opened before us. Coming near the rim, I
fell upon my hands and knees, awe-struck, and crept
cautiously to the rocky brink; for with all my natural
and acquired courage, I was unwilling at once to walk up
to the giddy verge, and look down upon the noisy, fiery

gulf beneath my feet. Shortly, however, I was able to stand very near and gaze upon this wonder of the world, which I wish I could set before my readers in all its mystery, magnitude, and grandeur.

" It is not a lofty cone, or mountain-top pointing to the heavens, but a vast chasm in the earth, five or six times the depth of Niagara Falls, and seven or eight miles in circumference. It is situated on the flank of a vast mountain, which has been gradually piled up by a similar agency during the course of ages. Such is the extent and depth of Kilauea, that it would take in, entire, the city of Philadelphia or New York, and make their loftiest spires, viewed from the rim, appear small and low. * * * While through the eye the impressions of grandeur, strong at first, increased till the daylight was gone. The impressions received through the ear were peculiar, and by no means inconsiderable. The fiercely whizzing sound of gas and steam rushing with varying force through obstructed apertures in blowing cones, or cooling crusts of lava; the labouring, wheezing, struggling, as of a living mountain, breathing fire and smoke and sulphurous gas from his lurid nostrils, tossing up molten rocks or detached portions of fluid lava, and breaking up vast indurated masses with varied detonations—all impressively bade us stand in awe. When we reached the verge, or whenever we came from a little distance to look over, these strange sounds increased, as if some intelligent power, with threatening tones and gestures, indignant at our obtrusiveness, were forbidding our approach. The effect of this on aboriginal visitors, before the true God was made known to them, may have been to induce or confirm the superstition that a deity or family of deities dwelt there, recognized the movements of men, and in various ways expressed anger against them. * * * The surface of this body of lava is subject to unceasing changes from year to year; for ' deep calleth unto deep,' and the billows of this troubled ocean ' cannot rest.' As night approached, we took our station on the north side, on the

very brink, where we supposed we should be able the
most securely and satisfactorily to watch the action of
this awful laboratory during the absence of the light of
the sun.   Though the spot where we spread our blanket
for a lodgement had been considered as the safest in the
neighbourhood, there was room for the feeling of inse-
curity. * * * The mass which supported us had doubtless
been shaken a thousand times, and was very liable every
hour to be shaken again ; but being in the short curvature
of the crater, like the keystone of an arch, it could not
easily be thrown from its position by any agitation that
would naturally occur while this great safety-valve is kept
open ; or the numerous fissures around it, reaching to the
bowels of the mountain, convey harmlessly from unknown
depths, gases, and volumes of steam, generated where
water comes in contact with intense volcanic heat.   Our
position was about four thousand feet above the level of
the sea, and one thousand above the surface of the lake.
The great extent of the surface of the lava lake, the
numerous places in it where the fiery element was displaying itself, the conical mouths here and there
discharging glowing lava, overflowing and spreading its
waves around, or belched out in detached and molten
masses that were shot forth with detonations, perhaps
by the force of gases struggling through from below the
surface, while the vast column of vapour and smoke
ascended up towards heaven, and the coruscations of
the emitted, brilliant lava illuminated the clouds that
passed over the terrific gulf—all presented by night a
splendid and sublime panorama of volcanic action, probably nowhere else surpassed. * * *

" After gazing at the wonderful phenomenon some
twenty hours, taking but a little time for repose, I found
the sense of fear subside, and curiosity prompt to a closer
intercourse with Pele, and a more familiar acquaintance
with her doings and habits.   Many who try the experi-
ment, though at first appalled, are ready, after a few
hours, to wend their way down the steep sides of the

crater. Thus we descended into the immense pit from
the north-east side, where it was practicable, first to the
black ledge, or amphitheatre gallery, and thence to the
surface of the lava lake. This we found extremely irregular, presenting cones, mounds, plains, vast bridges
of lava recently cooled, pits and caverns, and portions
of considerable extent in a moveable and agitated state.
We walked over lava, which by some process had been
fractured into immensely large slabs, as though it had
been contracted by cooling or been heaved up irregularly
by the semi-fluid mass below. In the fissures of this
fractured lava the slabs or blocks two feet below the
surface were red-hot. A walking-stick thrust down
would flame instantly.

"Passing over many such masses of lava, we ventured
towards the more central part of the lake, and came near
to a recent mound, which had probably been raised on
the cooling surface, after our arrival the day before.
From the top of it flowed melted lava, which spread
itself in waves to a considerable distance on one side,
then on the other, all around. The masses thrown out
in succession moved sluggishly, and as they flowed down
the inclined plane, a crust was formed over them, darkened
and hardened, and became stationary, while the stream
moved below it. The front of the mass, red-hot, pressed
along down, widening and expending itself, and forcing
itself through a net-work, as it were, of irregular filaments
of iron, which the cooling process freely supplied. This
motion of a flowing mass, whether larger or smaller, seen
from the rim of the crater by night, gives the appearance
of a fiery surf, or a rolling wave of fire, or the dancing
along of an extended semi-circular flame on the surface
of the lake. When one wave has expended itself, or
found its level, or otherwise become stationary, another
succeeds and passes over it in like manner, and then
another, sent out, as it were, by the pulsations of the
earth's open artery at the top of the mound. This
shows how a mound, cone, pyramid, or mountain can

be gradually built of lava, and wide plains covered at
its base with the same material.

"We approached near the border of some of these
waves, and reached the melted lava with a stick two
yards long, and thus did gross violence to Pele's taba.
I thus obtained several specimens red-hot from the flowing mass. I have since had occasion to be surprised at
the absence of fear in this close contiguity with the terrible
element, where the heat under our feet was as great as
our shoes would bear, and the radiating heat from the
moving mass was so intense that I could face it but a
few seconds at a time at the distance of two or three
yards. Yet having carefully observed its movements a
while, I threw a stick of wood upon the thin crust of a
moving wave where I believed it would bear me, even if
it should bend a little, and stood upon it a few moments.
In that position, thrusting my cane down through the
cooling, tough crust about half an inch thick, I withdrew
it, and forthwith there gushed up of the melted, flowing
lava under my feet enough to form a globular mass two
and a half or three inches in diameter, which, as it cooled,
I broke off, and bore away as spoils from the ancient
domain and favourite seat of the Diana of the Hawaiians.
Parts in violent action we dared not approach. There
is a remarkable variety in the volcanic productions of
Hawaii,—a variety as to texture, form, and size, from
the vast mountain and extended plain to the fine drawn
and most delicate vitreous fibre, the rough clinker, the
smooth stream, the basaltic rock, and masses compact
and hard as granite or flint; and the pumice, or porous
scoria or cinders, which, when hot, probably formed a
scum or foam on the surface of the denser molten mass.
Considerable quantities of capillary glass are produced at
Kilauea, though I am not aware that the article is found
elsewhere on the Islands. Its production has been deemed
mysterious. In its appearance it resembles human hair,
and is among the natives familiarly called 'Lanaho o
Pele'—the hair of Pele. It is formed, I presume, by

the tossing off of small detached portions of lava of the
consistence of melted glass from the mouths of cones,
when a fine vitreous thread is drawn out between the
moving portion and that from which it is detached.   The
fine spun product is then blown about by the wind, both
within and around the crater, and is collected in little
locks or tufts.   Sulphur is seen, but in small quantities,
in and around the crater, and at a little distance from the
rim are yellow banks on which beautiful crystals of sulphur may be found.   In one place, a pool of pure distilled
water, condensed from the steam that rises from a deep
fissure, affords the thirsty traveller a beverage far better
than that of the ordinary distiller.   There is, however, a
gas produced by the volcano, highly deleterious if breathed
often or freely,   This is one source of danger to the
visitor, which, while I was down a thousand feet below
the rim, produced a temporary coughing. * * *

"Kilauea may be regarded as one of the safety valves
of a bottomless reservoir of melted earth below the cooled
and cooling crust on which mountains rise, rivers flow, and
oceans roll, and cities are multiplied as the habitations of
men.   It has been kept open from time immemorial,
always displaying active power.   The circumambient air
which carries off the caloric, sometimes aided by the rain,
is incessantly endeavouring to shut this valve, or bridge
over this orifice of three or four square miles of the fiery
abyss.   Sometimes the imperfect bridge of cooling lava
is pierced with half a hundred rough, large, conical
chimneys, emitting gas, smoke, flame, and lava ; and
sometimes the vast bridge is broken up, and the cones
submerged, and probably fused again by the intense heat
of the vast fluid mass supplied fresh from the interior.
This mass rises gradually higher and higher, hundreds
of feet, till, by its immense pressure against the sides
of the crater, aided, perhaps, by the power of gas or
steam, it forces a passage for miles through the massive
walls, and inundates with its fiery deluge some portion
of the country below ; or passing through it as a river of

fire, pours itself into the sea at the distance of twenty-five miles, thus disturbing with awful uproar the domain of Neptune, and enlarging the dominions of the Hawaiian sovereign. The whole Island, with its ample and towering mountains, is often shaken with awful throes, and creation here 'groaneth and travaileth in pain.'

" In July, 1840, a river of lava flowed out from Kilauea, and, passing some miles under ground, burst out in the district of Puna, and inundated a portion of the country, sweeping down forests, and as a river, a mile wide, fell into the sea, heated the waters of the ocean, making war upon its inhabitants, and by the united action of this volcanic flood and the sea, formed several huge rough hills of sand and lava along the shore."

" Honolulu, 16th.—Finding that a barque called the ' Comet' is advertised to sail to San Francisco in a few days, we went to look at her accommodations this morning, and find them to be of a superior character, which has induced us to choose berths in her.

" 17th, first day.—At half-past nine we attended the native place of worship, which is a large old building situated at the opposite end of the town from the stone church. Going early, we seated ourselves at the foot of the stairs leading to the pulpit until the minister, L. Smith, arrived, who invited Father to sit beside him in the pulpit. After music and singing at intervals had been gone through three separate times, Father had opportunity to unburden his mind, commencing with the text, ' Say ye to the righteous, it shall be well with him; say ye to the wicked, it shall be ill with him.' * * *

" Second day, 18th.—It was agreed for us to have an interview with the King and Queen at ten a.m., so accompanied by R. Wylie, one of the King's ministers, we attended at the appointed hour. An armed sentinel admitted us into the spacious premises; but on approaching the palace an attendant informed us the King was sick. We sat down in one of the Queen's apartments, and sent a message to her, but all the answer we could get was that they were sick and asleep. Finding it useless to press the matter further, I left some small presents for the Queen and Prince, and we then withdrew. R. Wylie informed us that the King was subject to frequent attacks of asthma. We felt sorry not to have the opportunity of expressing our feelings of Christian interest on behalf of these young people.

" Honolulu, sixth day, 22nd.—The sailing of the 'Comet' has been put off until to-morrow morning, which has afforded opportunity for receiving and making various calls upon individuals. R. Wylie paid us a visit this morning, and expressed his entire unity with our visit, which he thought would be useful in removing an idea which had become prevalent that the Quakers had imbibed Unitarian doctrines. He informed us that the King had gone from home for some days, so we shall not be likely to see him. * * * It is quite a relief to have got through what seems to have been called for here, as the climate is very relaxing. It is said we have lost our colour since our arrival, and we are much thinner. The heat is not greater than we have felt elsewhere, but being continuous, is very relaxing to the system. The thermometer stands at 88° in the middle of the day, and the sun is directly over head.

" On board the barque ' Comet,' on her way to San Francisco, 23rd 6th mo., 1860.—Came on board this morning, with about twenty cabin passengers, thankful to leave the Sandwich Islands without being attacked by the fever to which new-comers are subject, which is described as being of a mild nature, and not often fatal. * The natives are naturally opposed to close employment; but love to eat and sleep much, and work little. Owing to the scarcity of whales, the whalers that used to call

for supplies are greatly fallen off, and there is not much
demand for general produce since California has come
under cultivation. Many invalids visit the Islands as a
last resource, and often find an early grave. There are
no serpents or venomous reptiles, with the exception of
a few centipedes. Frogs and toads are unknown. Birds
are scarce.

" First day, 5th 8th mo.— * * * We are now waiting
to receive orders to go on board the ' Lizzie Spalding,'
bound to Melbourne. The voyage is sometimes made in
two months, but vessels are occasionally three months
out. I hope you will often remember us in our floating
home, and pray for our preservation from the dangers of
the sea.

" San Francisco, 14th.—On board the ' Lizzie Spalding,' which is still at the wharf. Had calls from several
of our friends. Helen Pattin, whom we visited a few
days ago, brought us a basketful of apples, peaches,
oranges, and limes, and it seemed hard for her to
leave us.

" 3rd 9th month.—The monotony of everyday sea life
was broken in upon this morning by the appearance of a
shark following in the wake of our vessel, which was
captured by means of a cord and hook baited with meat.
After being speared, he was raised from deck, where he
floundered about for some time, striking fiercely with his
tail. He was six feet six inches long, and about as thick
as a man's body. Owing to light winds, we have made
slow progress during the last few days. Sometimes we
have only sailed at the rate of two miles an hour. Thermometer 82°.

" 18th.—We have met with the S.E. trade wind, and
are making good progress. The nights are trying, the
heat being about as great as in the day. We sat down

in our own room to hold our meeting on first day; but I was much tried with a spirit of heaviness, finding that although the spirit was willing, the flesh was scarcely under its control.

" 21st.—We have now a north wind which brings heat; but the evenings are pleasant, and we enjoy sitting upon deck, where the new moon sheds its beams over us, and our juvenile company are allowed to join us, and take exercise upon deck. Sometimes they unite in singing. Hitherto we have been able to make a pretty direct course, and expect to pass between the Navigator and Friendly Islands. I am frequently reminded of the language, ' They that go down to the sea in ships, that do business in great waters, these see the works of the Lord and His wonders in the deep.' I have never been at sea during a heavy gale, but it is interesting to mark how the ship meets the waves, and ploughs her way through the mighty waters, the swell being sometimes so great as to make her roll from side to side, whilst the waves have dashed over the lower deck. Truly the Lord hath been merciful unto us, making this voyage, which I dreaded in prospect, comparatively easy, and hitherto we have escaped sea-sickness. Thermometer 83°.

" 13th.—Nearly becalmed all night. Another shark was captured this morning about ten and a half feet in length. After being killed, he was hung outside the quarter-deck for inspection, and finally dropped into the sea again. An albatross, as large as a fine goose, was also taken by means of a baited hook. Its body was white, and its wings of a dark colour. When expanded, each wing is upwards of a yard long. It walked about without seeming alarmed; but it is not formed for walking freely, and cannot take wing from a flat surface. When our curiosity had been satisfied, it was restored to its native element.

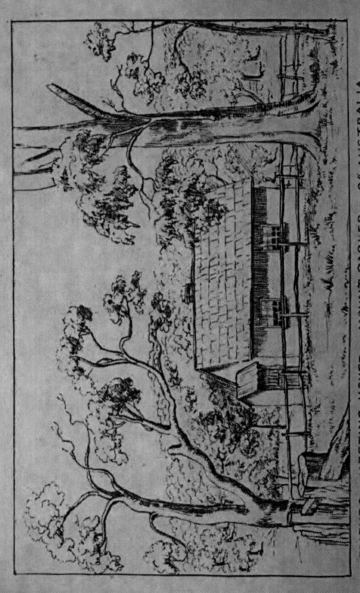

FRIENDS MEETING-HOUSE, MOUNT BARKER, S? AUSTRALIA.

" Melbourne, Australia, 10th mo. 80th.— * * * We remained on board all night, and this morning Charles Mould and James Hope came to welcome us, having seen a notice of our arrival in the newspaper. A custom house officer came on board, saw our luggage, and asked if we had any contraband goods, mentioning tobacco, and on being answered in the negative, he gave us a pass, which no one asked to see afterwards. Being some distance from the wharf, we hired a boat, into which we were let down in an arm chair. During our voyage of seventy-five days we have met with great kindness from Captain Ames and his agreeable wife, and have had no trouble from our fellow-passengers, in some of whom we have felt much interested. After landing at the wharf, we came three miles by rail to this city, and were conducted to the house of Charles Mould, where we found a welcome from his wife.

" 3rd 1st month.—Our friends not having made arrangements for visits to-day, we took the opportunity of walking to the Botanical Gardens, which lay near us. The way there was through a large park, several of which are reserved in various parts around the city. There are some large native trees, and others have been planted. The gardens are laid out with taste, and kept in the neatest order. They are bounded on one side by a marsh and native shrubs. Black swans and other fowls were swimming in the water, and feathered songsters flying from tree to tree warbling their varied notes. There is an aviary, and cages of foreign birds, monkeys, &c. The greenhouse contains various tropical plants, and there are a great variety of native trees, shrubs, and plants in the gardens.

" Launceston, 1st 12th month.—Went on board the ' Black Swan' on fifth day morning, and after a voyage, rendered suffering by sea-sickness, we entered the mouth of the River Tamar, a very winding stream, with

picturesque scenery along its banks, between three and
four o'clock yesterday afternoon; but the wind and tide
being against us, together with frequent delays from
coming in contact with sandbanks, and having to wait
for the tide rising, we did not reach the wharf until
midnight; so remained on board all night. Rose early
this morning, and took up our quarters at the Criterion
Hotel. After breakfast we drove six miles in a hired
carriage to the house of the only member of our Society
that Father knew of in this neighbourhood. The country
through which we passed was hilly, and the uplands
densely wooded with a small growth of gum and acacia
trees. The cleared land looked very verdant, and the
hedges being chiefly composed of wild rose bushes and
yellow broom in full flower, have a very gay appearance.
The acacias are also in bloom, and give a fragrant
smell. * * * In the afternoon we had a call from
Francis Cotton, who happened to be in town.

" Hobart Town, 4th 12th month.—On asking for our
bill at the hotel before leaving Launceston, we found the
charges higher than we have before met with in all our
travels. Took the coach on second day morning at five
o'clock, and after a long day's journey of one hundred
and twenty miles across the Island, reached this place
about eight o'clock last night. Our kind friend Frederic
Mackie was waiting our arrival, and on entering his house
we met with a kind welcome from his amiable and valuable
wife. The central part of the journey from Launceston
to Hobart Town is not very interesting; but the road is
good, having been made by the convicts in the early
settlement of the Island. When within ten miles of
Hobart Town the country improves and becomes very
picturesque. The river Derwent, with its little verdant
islands, flows in a serpentine course at the foot of the
mountains, and the neighbourhood is scattered over with
country seats. There having been more rain than usual
this spring, vegetation is very luxuriant, and the wild

roses, acacias, and flowering brooms, together with
garden hedges of geraniums, sweetbriar, and here and
there a weeping willow, give a pleasing effect to the
whole.

" 10th.—Had two sittings of the Yearly Meeting, and
got through most of the business in a harmonious manner.
After hearing the new advices and queries read, Francis
Cotton remarked that he had previously felt a little pre-
judiced; but he believed that Friends had had an eye to
the truth, and to the glory of God. It was quite gratifying
to find general satisfaction with the alterations. A committee was appointed to prepare an Epistle to the Meeting
for Sufferings.

" 11th.—Breakfasted at Thomas Crouch's, who is
the deputy sheriff. * * * We had an open and favoured
religious opportunity with the family. We afterwards
went into a small cottage with a sloping roof, and so
low that we had to stoop on entering the door. At one
end of a room about seven feet wide and fourteen feet
long was a shoemaker's bench, and utensils belonging
to the trade. At the other end was a fireplace with a
somewhat smoky chimney, on each side of which, and
under the window, a good supply of firewood was stowed.
The furniture consisted of a few chairs, a stool, a small
table, and some shelves containing crockery ware. How
was my heart humbled and contrited in hearing the occu-
pant of this humble abode express how thankful he felt
for the blessings bestowed upon him! * * * He was from
Stafford, where his father was in the habit of attending
Friends' meetings, and he spoke of the piety of some of
his brothers and sisters, and said he had been the wildest
of his family; but latterly the Lord had opened his eyes,
and given him to see things in a different light. He had
suffered from unreasonable men, and now kept much
alone. About three months since he married a Scotch-
woman. With this interesting couple we partook of the

stream which at seasons waters the heritage of God, and gave expression to the exercise of our minds.

" Kelvedon, Tasmania, second day, 24th 12th month, 1860.—After commending each other to the care of Israel's Shepherd, we took leave of our dear friends F. and R. A. Mackie at six o'clock this morning, Henry Propstring driving us in his own carriage. After proceeding a few miles, we crossed the river Derwent in a flat, and passing through the neat little town of Richmond, our road lay in a winding course round the hills and deep ravines along a densely wooded valley. Reached Runymede, the estate of a merchant in Hobart Town, at one p.m., having travelled about thirty miles. This is a fine farm and sheep run of thirty thousand acres, with a good house, outbuildings, gardens, &c. We found Joseph Cotton awaiting our arrival with horses for the rest of the journey; so after taking a lunch of bacon and bread, with good milk, we drove twelve miles, chiefly through the bush, on a rough and mountainous road, heading deep ravines, and passing through intervening valleys. On reaching Prosser's Plains, we took up our quarters at Thomas Crittenden's, whose establishment is like a little colony. * * * They have a sheep and dairy farm of several thousand acres, and spoke of having three thousand five hundred sheep to shear this year.

" Fourth day.—Set out again at eight a.m., when our road lay through a very stony, rugged, and mountainous district. We crossed Prosser's River three times, the water in the last place reaching to the body of the horse. After alighting to rest by the riverside, our horses were led, whilst we walked upon a narrow track over large and small rough stones at the foot of a high, rocky mountain where the road had been swept away. Soon after remounting, we sighted Prosser's Bay. Maria Island, with its lofty mountain in the centre, and small hamlet called Darlington at its foot, gives increasing interest to the landscape. The forests present a somewhat gloomy aspect, on account of the trees having cast their bark. They are chiefly evergreen, and consist of the gum, peppermint, heoak, sheoak, wattle, wild cherry, &c. I noticed some grass trees just rising from the ground. Weary and faint, we arrived at Sand Spit, where we were taken to a good farmhouse called Rhebens, situated on a fine Bay, about two o'clock, having ridden twenty miles. I was glad to lie down to rest after dinner, and in the evening we had a ramble on the shore. A person called Grubber rents the farm, which consists of nine thousand acres. There is some good land in the valleys, but the mountains are only fit for sheep runs. One sheep requires an acre of land for support. The farmers are now engaged in sheep shearing. The yield from a sheep is about three pounds of wool, the present price of which is one shilling and eightpence per pound. The merino sheep are the kind kept here. They are small compared with our English sheep.

" Fifth day.—Arose feeling very faint and weary, so father left me to rest whilst he went to see two of F. Cotton's sons who have lately commenced farming in the bush about two miles from here. Left Sand Spit at two o'clock, and rode fifteen miles to Spring Bay, where we were kindly received at the house of a person of the name of Rudd.

" Sixth day.—At nine a.m. we set out and pursued our journey, which lay chiefly among the bush where the country was less mountainous. We crossed several creeks, and had to pick our way among fallen timber. Halted at noon, and got some refreshment at a small hotel; but as usual in travelling on this Island, we did not meet with either good bread or good water. On starting again our horses had to wade through Swan River, which was more than knee deep. About six p.m. reached the house of Francis Cotton. Sloping woodlands skirt the valley, and

N

in front of the house there are gravel walks, flower beds,
shrubberies, &c., beyond which is the sea. Maria Island
and other mountains bound one of the most beautiful
situations which could well be chosen. Having performed a journey of twenty-eight miles on horseback
to-day, I feel less fatigued than might have been expected ; although we mostly ride at walking pace.

" 24th 1st month, 1861.—Left Abraham Davey's
yesterday afternoon ; lodged at an hotel, and having
hired a spring cart and a driver, left Campbelltown at
six o'clock this morning. Breakfasted at Appin, a nice
little village ten miles on our way. The rest of the journey of sixteen miles was on an open road through the
bush, along the ridge of the Wollongong mountain. After
crossing the rocky bed of the London river, we met a man
on horseback, who, in answer to enquiries respecting the
road, informed us that we should have to pass through a
bog four miles long, where the mud would reach up to
the axletree of our carriage. This was discouraging, and
we were almost tempted to return ; but thought it best
to see for ourselves, and although the difficulty of getting
along had been overrated, it was all the horse could do
to pull the empty carriage through the mud whilst we,
with the help of long sticks to balance ourselves, had to
creep amongst the bushes, where the brambles seemed
as if they would tear the clothes from my back. Some
hundred feet below us lay the ocean, of which we now
and then had a peep through the trees. After getting
through the bog, we had to descend a rugged, long, and
very steep mountain, down which we were obliged to
walk. The foliage around us was very rich, with here
and there a cabbage tree with its bare trunk as straight
as an arrow shooting up to the height of sixty or eighty
feet. The foliage is in fan-shaped tufts of long leaves at
the top of the tree. The leaves are used for straw hats,
and although high in price, are neither handsome nor
durable. We also noticed many fern and grass trees.

FRIEND'S MEETING-HOUSE, DEVONSHIRE ST SYDNEY.

About four p.m. we sighted George Cox's house, where we found a welcome. * * *

"25th, 1st mo.—There are many orange trees on Dr. Cox's premises well filled with fruit, which is green at present, and does not ripen until the fifth month. We also saw many lemon trees; but the fruit is of an inferior kind. The vines were laden with clusters of grapes, and two large India fig, or Indiarubber trees, with their long, smooth, myrtle-shaped evergreen leaves, were beautiful to look upon. A neighbouring orchard of orange trees, covering one acre of ground, was pointed out to us which yielded an income of three hundred pounds per annum.

"26th, seventh day.—Arose early, breakfasted, and at six a.m. took an affectionate leave of the family, and set out on our return to Abraham Davey's, accompanied by Dr. Cox on horseback. On arriving at the foot of the mountain, a yoke of oxen, which our friends had engaged, were in readiness to attach to our carriage to help us along. After getting through the boggy road we dismissed the oxen, and Dr. Cox left us. We halted, and lunched by the river side, and rested a little at Appin, arriving at Campbelltown about four p.m., where we changed horses, and reached our place of destination in safety and in peace. Thus are we constrained to set up an Ebenezer to the Lord's praise, who hath protected us from harm during this arduous journey.

"Bathurst, 5th 2nd month.—As your dear father felt drawn to visit an individual who resides more than one hundred and fifty miles from Sydney, we rose early yesterday morning, and at half-past six o'clock were seated in a railway carriage, and travelled fifteen miles to Paramatta, where we took the coach to Bathurst. The first nineteen miles of our journey was through a fertile and well settled country. Soon after passing the village of Penrith we crossed the Nepean River in a punt, and

ascended the Blue Mountains, where we found the roads
bad and rugged, and were informed, after travelling ten
miles, that what we had passed over was like a bowling
green compared to what we should have to encounter the
next twenty miles, and there was some truth in the remark.   About three p.m. the clouds, which had been
darkening around us, suddenly broke in fury over our
heads, and the wind arose, the thunder roared, the lightning flashed, and hailstones the size of large marbles,
and some oblong shaped, like a pullet's egg, rattled upon
the coach, and fell around us.   The hail soon gave place
to heavy rain, and although the stage professedly was a
covered one, with curtains around, the rain penetrated
through the roof and poured upon us.   I had only a sun
bonnet on my head, which I took off to wring, and to
prevent taking cold tied a handkerchief over my head.
After much tossing, and sitting in wet clothes for three
hours, we reached the hotel on Pulpit Hill, our lodging
place, having travelled about fifty miles by stage.   I took
off my wet clothes, and retired for the night, after drinking
some hot gruel.   I did not sleep well, having a pain in
my head, consequent on the jerks we had had, which
many times raised us from our seats.   Were seated in
the stage again at six a.m. the next morning, and after
plunging through deep mud, came to a piece of good road
which was succeeded by rough, uneven, stony ground,
like the bed of a rivulet, where we had to hold fast and
balance ourselves in order to keep our seats.   For many
miles, both yesterday and to-day, as far as the eye could
reach, nothing but the unbroken forest met our view, and
our four horses were driven often in a winding course
between the trees and stumps against which we were in
danger of striking.   We are informed that some of the
ravines upon these mountains are fifteen hundred feet
deep.   The heavily laden wool waggons drawn by ten
and twelve oxen each, on their way to Sydney, and the
merchants waggons with goods and provisions for the
country, we constantly see along our track.   Small hotels

GLENCOE   OR   HARDSCRABBLE. — V. D. L. —

are very numerous. The last sixteen miles of our
journey was over Bathurst Plains, and we reached the
town about seven p.m. wearied in body, but thankful for
the preserving care of our God whilst prosecuting one of
the most dangerous journeys that we have had. * * *

" Wattle Flatts, 6th.—Lodged at an hotel, and at six
o'clock this morning were on our way to this place in a
stage. We had to walk up a very steep mountain, where
it was enough for the horses to drag the carriage, and
unsafe for passengers to sit in it. About eleven a.m. we
came in sight of the Flatts, where there are gold mines,
on the river Turon. The country has an unsightly appearance. Some places reminded me of a graveyard,
being a succession of mounds and deep oblong holes.
We alighted at an hotel, and found the individual we
sought acting as engineer at a quartz crushing mill. He
has a wife and three children, who are living in a tent
until a cottage is erected for them. They seemed much
pleased to see us. The afternoon was very wet, and the
inner covering of the tent became saturated with moisture,
and the fire being outside, the thoughts of sleeping in a
tent about eight feet long, and where our heads, when
standing, nearly touched the ridge, was to me discouraging. In the evening we had a precious religious
opportunity with our friends, when much encouragement
flowed towards them in their isolated situation. Some
of the neighbours (many of whom lived in bark houses)
provided a shelter for our host and family, and their tent
was given up for our use during the night.

" 7th.—Arose before five o'clock, but on meeting the
coach, were disappointed to find it quite full; but after
some hours spent in search of a vehicle to take us to
Bathurst, our host found a man and a horse and cart,
so taking an affectionate leave of our friends, we commenced our journey. In the course of conversation, we
learned that our driver had been in the employ of my

grandfather James Hall. We had a jolting drive, and a
hot walk down the steep mountain. On approaching the
town, two forks of the Macquarie River, which we had
crossed the previous day, were much swollen, and I feared
the horse would be taken off his feet; but we were
enabled to get through safely, and took up our quarters
at an hotel.

" Melbourne, Victoria, 27th 3rd month, 1861.—Paid
farewell visits to several families at Emerald Hill and St.
Kilda. The evening meeting was well attended, and was
a season of deep feeling and solemnity. Father addressed
us from the parting words of the Apostle Paul to the
elders of the church at Ephesus: ' Take heed to your-
selves and to the flock over which the Holy Ghost hath
made you overseers,' &c. Robert Lumsden and Samuel
Levitt afterwards gave expression to the exercise of their
minds, and I felt constrained to bow the knee and suppli-
cate for the Lord's blessing. The parting from some of
our dear friends whose countenances we may never see
again upon earth, was affecting; but how consoling is
the humble trust that through the merits and mediation
of the Saviour, we may meet again where partings are no
more."

My father feeling discharged from further service in
the Southern Hemisphere, made enquiries about several
vessels ready to leave for London. At this time steamers
did not ply between Melbourne and London, and the
regular sailing passenger ships went round Cape Horn.
They took berths finally in one of Green's vessels, called
the "Agincourt."

" 28th.—Got all our heavy luggage on board the ' Agincourt,' and in the afternoon Charles Mould went with us
to the Museum, which occupies four large rooms in the
University, a large and noble building in the suburbs of

the city. The surrounding grounds contain forty acres,
which are being laid out as pleasure grounds, and some
of it as an elaborate botanical garden. The museum
contains a great variety of native and foreign specimens
of quadrupeds, birds, fishes, fossils, shells, insects, eggs,
sponges, seeds, &c., &c., with models of the gold fields,
mining operations, and machinery in use. Both the
grounds and museum are open to the public gratis.

" 30th.—Came on board the 'Agincourt' about noon,
accompanied by our kind friend James Prince. Samuel
Levitt, Walter Brown, and William Cooper afterwards
came in boats to see us. At six p.m. the anchor was
raised, and we were assisted up the Bay by a steam tug,
but anchored within for the night.

" 5th 4th month.—We have not suffered much from
sea-sickness. There are about two hundred passengers
on board, twenty of whom are in the first class cabins.
Captain Tickel is commander. There are five mates,
eight young midshipmen, and thirty common sailors.
Before we left the wharf at Melbourne a very painful
circumstance occurred. A man came on board whose
wife and three children had had their passage paid to
London. It appeared that the husband had been an
intemperate character, and had ill-treated his wife, who
along with her children was deserting him. After trying
in vain to detain his wife, he got possession of his little
boy, and remained on board the ship for some time after
she sailed, a small boat accompanying the vessel to carry
them back. At length the child was taken from the
father by force, and he being tied with ropes, was let
down into the boat. This affair cast a deep gloom over
my mind, under the renewed feeling that I was in a world
of sin and sorrow, and I longed for the wings of a dove
that I might flee away and be at rest.

" 25th 6th month.—Still favoured with a brisk wind,

and made two hundred and sixty-eight miles yesterday, which is the greatest distance we have made in one day since leaving Melbourne. Father keeps a daily account of our progress, from which it appears that the distance from Melbourne to Cape Horn is seven thousand miles, and from thence to the Equator is six thousand miles, and from the Equator to the shores of Old England is supposed to be about four thousand miles. Some of our first class passengers are frivolous and volatile kind of people, of loose moral character, whose loud laughter often annoys us; but we esteem it a favour they are not in the habit of swearing. The only female who seems at all companionable for me is Madame Cotton, a French lady, who speaks broken English. From eight to ten o'clock at night is generally spent in playing at cards. We feel the time somewhat tedious, and the nights trying from the heat. My dear husband has not felt it required of him to hold public meetings on board, but has distributed tracts, which have been well received. There is a converted Jew here who is a Scripture reader, and who seems to be an interesting character. We find the N.E. trade wind stronger than the S.E., and have made two hundred and fifty-nine miles to-day, just clearing the tropics, where we have been for twenty-nine days. We are now north of the sun, which has been vertical to-day, and we have had no lengthened shadow. The days are increasing in length, a most agreeable change from the long dreary nights which we had after reaching Cape Horn. I generally rise at six a.m., and have been engaged in looking over and correcting my home journal. We have finished reading the Old Testament through, and have now begun the New Testament.

" 24th 7th month.—On awaking at half-past one a.m. we heard unusual noises, and on looking out of the window found we were just entering the dock at Blackwall. Thus have we been permitted, through the tender mercies

of our God, once more to set our feet upon the shores of
our native land in safety and in peace after an absence
of nearly four years. Under a sense of the Lord's goodness towards His unworthy children, the language hath
been raised in my heart, 'My soul doth magnify the
Lord, and my spirit hath rejoiced in God my Saviour;
for He that is mighty hath done for me great things, and
holy is His name.'

" Before leaving the ship, we were agreeably surprised
to see our son Thomas come on board, and to learn that
our daughters and other relatives were in usual health.
We took up our quarters at Joseph Armfield's, where
many kind friends came to greet and welcome us home
again, with whom it is a great treat to mingle in social
converse. Surely we may adopt the language, ' Return
unto thy rest, oh my soul! for the Lord hath dealt
bountifully with thee.' Something like the hundredfold
hath been witnessed in the sweet feeling of peace which
hath been granted in addition to many outward blessings,
which are given us richly to enjoy."

LATTER YEARS.

A FEW months after our father's return home, two of my sisters were married, and in the beginning of 1862 he removed with his remaining family to Manchester, where he believed it his duty to go and reside. He here too continued his active work for his Master, visiting the meetings comprised in Hardshaw West Monthly Meeting, and paying family visits to all the Friends. He was accompanied by his wife in this service. His health now began to fail, and weakness of the heart became apparent. In order to have the benefit of country air, and by the doctor's advice, we removed to Sale in Cheshire, about five miles out of Manchester, where there was a meeting of Friends. My father much enjoyed the sight of the green fields and trees, and was able to get out a good deal in a Bath chair. But his strength perceptibly failed, and after about three weeks of intense suffering at times, he quietly passed away in his easy chair in the sixth month of 1863, aged sixty-two years. He was interred in the Friends burial ground at Ashton-on-Mersey.

He was not able to recline in bed, from frequent difficulty of breathing. During his illness he spoke much of the love and mercy of God in Christ Jesus.

A few days before his death he wished us all to meet in his room, when he addressed us very beautifully, and bade us all farewell. He said after spending a morning of suffering mentally and bodily, but being now relieved, he wished to give utterance to some of his feelings on our account. He said some among us had been tenderly visited by the dayspring from on high, and had felt the peace of believing. He hoped such would keep steadfast, and persevere in dedicating themselves unto the Lord. We must trust in the Lord in all things, and bring all our burdens and sorrows before Him. It was his prayer that we might all meet on the right hand of God, and there unite in ascribing unto Him thanksgiving and praise. He felt he had fallen far short of what was required of him, and he trusted solely in the sacrifice of Jesus, and in the free mercy of God. He knew not how long he might remain here, but we could not wish for his continuance: that our hearts could not be sufficiently contrited in contemplating the love and mercy of God shewn in the offering of His dear Son. Finally he committed and commended us to the grace of our Lord Jesus Christ, and said, " Farewell, farewell." He then called us each to him, and bade us farewell individually. He had great difficulty in speaking throughout, and was often overcome by sobs.

My mother lived thirteen years after the death of her husband, being seventy-one years old when she died. Her health during this time was never good, as several other family bereavements united in impairing her strength ; but she was always cheerful and happy. Even when alone she never felt lonely, saying she could hold communion with her Father in Heaven, and her countenance often showed the sweet peace she enjoyed. She had great pleasure in the company of her young grandchildren, one of whom she generally had staying with her.

When unable to go out, she thought she might do a little good by sending packets of tracts through the post to those she believed would appreciate them. She much enjoyed the lovely country around Taunton, where she went to reside about three years after her husband's decease. She lived there about seven years, and on her son's giving up his business there she removed to Worcester, where she had three grandchildren, the death of whose mother she had keenly felt a few years before. Here the last three years of her life were spent. Increased feebleness was apparent, and she could not bear much exertion; but was able frequently to enjoy a drive in the warm weather. During the last six months of her life she suffered much from repeated attacks of asthma, which no remedies we could apply seemed to relieve, and on the seventeenth of third month, 1876, she passed peacefully to her heavenly rest, and was interred in the Friends burial ground at Worcester.

During the last three weeks, when she was entirely confined to bed, in the midst of intense pain, she seemed so happy, she did not know how to express herself, and was praising God, and blessing Him for all His goodness, and even sometimes singing. She said she felt she must praise her Heavenly Father aloud. She enjoyed hearing hymns read and sung to her, particularly Samuel Rutherford's last words, and she often repeated some of the lines.

" The sands of time are sinking,
   The dawn of Heaven breaks,
The summer morn I've sighed for,
   The fair, sweet morn awakes.
Dark, dark hath been the midnight,
   But dayspring is at hand ;
And glory, glory dwelleth
   In Emanuel's land."

She often said, " Oh! death, where is thy sting? oh grave, where is thy victory?" Her face after death bore the expression of most perfect peace and happiness.

JOHN BELL AND CO., PRINTERS, NEWCASTLE-ON-TYNE.